Let me be honest: my heart
prayer is that I'd rather spen.........
about it. As I was reading *When Prayer Is a Struggle*, however, I felt
as if I had a friend leading me, on a path, to pray more, to pray better, to pray until I could pray. I just couldn't put it down, except to
pause regularly to pray about a particular truth or with the prayers
at the end of every chapter. Before I started, I wasn't aware of how
much I needed the wisdom in this book. More importantly, I now
feel motivated (and more prepared) to spend more time before
the throne. And for that, I'm so thankful to the Lord for moving
Kevin to write this.

—**Jairo Namnún**, Director for International Coalitions, The
Gospel Coalition

How often I have reached toward my bookcase for a book on
prayer, only to pivot to another volume. What's that about? Guilt
. . . shame . . . embarrassment over my pathetic prayer life. Books
that are written by prayer masters too often intimidate rather
than inspire me. Kevin Halloran's *When Prayer Is a Struggle* has
had the opposite effect on my soul. Here's a fellow traveler—a
fellow failure—who has identified obstacles (my obstacles) to
praying and provided a hope-filled way forward. Kevin is a wise
yet approachable coach who will encourage you to keep praying
and not lose heart.

—**Craig Parro**, President, WordPartners

A summary of the beginning and end of the Christian life might
be that "the righteous shall live by faith" (Rom. 1:17). And for an
explanation of the essence of that life of faith, one can do no better than that of Calvin, who writes that "the chief exercise of faith
is prayer." So what do Christians do when we struggle to pray?
Does it mean that our faith is inadequate when this happens? The
resounding answer is *no*. Kevin Halloran, as a fellow struggler,

identifies some of the obstacles we face to the exercising of our faith through a life of prayer, and he guides us in how we can overcome those struggles. This is not just another book about prayer; rather, it is intended to be a Spirit-prompted aid to fostering and nourishing prayer. I recommend that you first read through the book prayerfully while pondering the questions about each of the obstacles to prayer that it tackles. And then I encourage you to do the same with another Christian or in a small group. In the Lord's kindness, may this book be used to bear the fruit of a life of prayer in its readers.

—**Gregory C. Strand**, Executive Director of Theology and Credentialing, Evangelical Free Church of America; Adjunct Professor of Pastoral Theology, Trinity Evangelical Divinity School

Prayer is one of the greatest privileges and weapons that we have as believers—and it's also one of the things that the enemy most seeks to distract, discourage, and derail us from. And, despite the fact that prayer struggles are common to man, we often feel alone in them. For that reason, we've been encouraged and blessed by Kevin Halloran's down-to-earth, relatable, and practically helpful approach to addressing the most typical hindrances to our prayer lives—and to addressing how we can grow to see prayer as a gift and joy rather than a duty or struggle. Whatever the state of your prayer life may be, you will find yourself somewhere in the pages of this book—and you will be encouraged and challenged to experience the depth and richness of communing with your heavenly Father.

—**Jeff and Sarah Walton**, Authors, *Together Through the Storms: Biblical Encouragements for Your Marriage When Life Hurts*

Prayer is a challenge for me, as it is for most Christians—probably because we fail to fully feel just how dependent we are on God.

Kevin Halloran's book offers a wise combination of theological reflection and practical helps—both of which are intended to drive us to our knees in prayer to the One who knows and loves us.

—**Trevin Wax**, General Editor, The Gospel Project; Author, *Rethink Your Self*, *This Is Our Time*, and *Gospel-Centered Teaching*

When Prayer Is a Struggle truly is a practical guide that helps us to connect, or reconnect, to the heart of the Father. Kevin honestly shares his own journey while asking us to consider our relationship with God and with others through prayer. I was challenged once again to pray the Word through Kevin's encouragement. His excellent, thought-provoking questions at the end of each section help us to explore the heart of the matter. Helpful, insightful, and timely for each of us—and especially for the world in which we live today. Well done, brother!

—**Mickey Weston**, Executive Director, Unlimited Potential Inc.; Former Major League Baseball Pitcher

Kevin's book on prayer is incredibly heartfelt. He is a praying person, and it makes me want to be a prayerful person too. Offering us practical wisdom for growing in the discipline of prayer, Kevin writes with a pastoral heart and an obvious love for God. I now have several takeaways that I'm eager to use when I pray!

—**Kristen Wetherell**, Author, *Fight Your Fears*; Coauthor, *Hope When It Hurts*

when
prayer
is a
struggle

when prayer is a struggle

A PRACTICAL GUIDE
FOR OVERCOMING
OBSTACLES IN PRAYER

kevin p. halloran

R&R
PUBLISHING
P.O. BOX 817 • PHILLIPSBURG • NEW JERSEY 08865-0817

© 2021 by Kevin P. Halloran

All rights reserved. No part of this book may be reproduced, stored in a retrieval system, or transmitted in any form or by any means—electronic, mechanical, photocopy, recording, or otherwise—except for brief quotations for the purpose of review or comment, without the prior permission of the publisher, P&R Publishing Company, P.O. Box 817, Phillipsburg, New Jersey 08865-0817.

Unless otherwise indicated, Scripture quotations are from the ESV® Bible (The Holy Bible, English Standard Version®), copyright © 2001 by Crossway, a publishing ministry of Good News Publishers. Used by permission. All rights reserved.

Scripture quotations marked (NASB) are from the New American Standard Bible® (NASB), Copyright © 1960, 1962, 1963, 1968, 1971, 1972, 1973, 1975, 1977, 1995 by The Lockman Foundation. Used by permission. www.Lockman.org

Scripture quotations marked (NIV) are taken from the Holy Bible, New International Version®, NIV®. Copyright © 1973, 1978, 1984, 2011 by Biblica, Inc.™ Used by permission of Zondervan. All rights reserved worldwide. www.zondervan.com. The "NIV" and "New International Version" are trademarks registered in the United States Patent and Trademark Office by Biblica, Inc.™

Italics within Scripture quotations indicate emphasis added.

Printed in the United States of America

Library of Congress Cataloging-in-Publication Data

Names: Halloran, Kevin P., author.
Title: When prayer is a struggle : a practical guide for overcoming
    obstacles in prayer / Kevin P. Halloran.
Description: Phillipsburg, New Jersey : P&R Publishing, 2021. | Includes
    bibliographical references. | Summary: "If you struggle to pray, be encouraged--God
wants to help you in your struggle. Led by God's Word and empowered by His Spirit,
you can addressthe obstacles to prayer by facing them head-on"--
    Provided by publisher.
Identifiers: LCCN 2021008302 | ISBN 9781629958750 (paperback) | ISBN
    9781629958767 (epub) | ISBN 9781629958774 (mobi)
Subjects: LCSH: Prayer--Christianity.
Classification: LCC BV215 .H3385 2021 | DDC 248.3/2--dc23
LC record available at https://lccn.loc.gov/2021008302

To God's praying people

"The prayer of the upright is His delight"
(Prov. 15:8 NASB)

contents

foreword

On a scale of 1 to 10, how would you rate your prayer life?

If yours is a 10, you probably don't need this book. You must already be seeking God with passion, persistence, and persuasion on behalf of your family, your church, and our world.

This book is for the rest of us.

Since you have opened this book, I assume that you are not a 10—and that you are interested in getting help with your prayer life. You are not alone.

One of the privileges and responsibilities entrusted to a pastor is that of meeting with members of his congregation to offer them practical help and encouragement. But here's what I found, through doing this: sometimes when people meet with a pastor, they don't know what to say, and so they fill the time with general conversation. How could I, as a pastor, open the door to an interaction that would be of lasting spiritual value?

Some years ago, I devised a list of topics that I thought people might like to discuss with their pastor. I wrote out questions on the front of envelopes, which I then filled with cards that offered various possible answers to them.

Now when I meet with a member of my congregation, I sometimes begin by saying, "We have an hour together, so let's make the best use of this time. If you have something you'd like to talk about, we can do that. If not, I have some suggestions written on these envelopes. You could choose one that might interest you."

Most times, people ask to see the envelopes.

The issues that are marked on the front of them include doctrine, effective witnessing, growth in Christian maturity, relationships with other believers, and Christian ministry. But there is another envelope that has been, without question, the most popular. I reckon that over the years, 80 percent of the people who have looked at the envelopes have chosen the one that asks, "How would you describe your prayer life?"

When they open this envelope and pull out the cards inside, each bears a word or two that might describe a person's prayer life: *Enjoyable, Hard Work, Valuable, Irregular, Unstructured, Aimless, A Failure.*

It is fascinating to watch how people process these cards. Spreading them out on the table, most people go through a process of elimination. "Well, it's not a failure. But I wouldn't say it's enjoyable, either. . . ." Most often, they choose two of the cards: "Irregular" and "Aimless."

People are looking for help—and if you are one of them, this book is for you. Kevin Halloran has brought together a treasure chest of wise and practical counsel that will deepen your prayers.

Kevin will help you bring structure and purpose to your prayer life. He will show you how to use any sense of failure you feel so that it helps, rather than hinders, your prayers. This book will expand your horizons and give you a new vision for how you can engage more effectively in prayer.

May God use it to bless and encourage you.

Colin S. Smith
Senior Pastor, The Orchard
President, Unlocking the Bible

introduction:
the struggle is real

"Everyone struggles to pray. Is a good prayer life even possible?"

I regretted those words as soon as they left my mouth. I knew that such a thought reflected a shallow view of God, of His gospel, and of prayer. And yet I had just blurted it out in front of our entire Bible study group!

While avoiding eye contact with others for a few minutes, I reflected on what I had said. Even though I knew my words were wrong, they reflected what I had felt for a long time. I had had many ups and downs in pursuing God through prayer. I was frustrated. A good sermon or book would encourage me for a few days or weeks, but then I'd drift back to where I had started and feel defeated by seemingly insurmountable obstacles. I had thought that attending seminary or holding leadership positions would fix this—but to no avail. Why did my growth in the daily discipline of prayer always sputter out?

Have you ever felt like I did? I suspect that you also struggle to pray if you picked up a book with this title. Maybe you've followed Christ for years; you love His Word and His church. But when it comes to prayer, you feel like a car stuck in mud. You make an effort, but your wheels are spinning and you're not going anywhere. You know there's more to God and the Christian life, but you aren't sure how to grow in prayer. You know the struggle to pray is real.

But did you know the struggle is also *good*?

THE STRUGGLE IS . . . GOOD

You heard me right. Think about it: you don't struggle to do what you want to avoid. For example, I don't struggle with the urge to light wads of my hard-earned cash on fire or take a sledgehammer to my car. I *do* sometimes struggle to exercise, even though I *desire* to be healthy. I *do* struggle to steward my money wisely, even though I do want to be faithful with what God has entrusted to me. Similarly, we all struggle to pray because *we have a desire to pray*. If we didn't have the desire, we wouldn't have a struggle.

The desire to pray isn't a given. When man rebelled in the garden of Eden, his sin cut him off from communion with God (see Gen. 3:8, 22–24). "Your iniquities have made a separation between you and your God," writes the prophet Isaiah, "and your sins have hidden his face from you so that he does not hear" (Isa. 59:2). The apostle Paul says similarly, "None is righteous, no, not one; no one understands; no one seeks for God" (Rom. 3:10–11; see also Psalm 14:1–3). Spiritually speaking, there is an infinite chasm between sinful humanity and a holy God. His face is hidden from sinners. He doesn't have to answer your prayer any more than you would have to do a favor for someone who betrayed you.

Thankfully, God sent His Son Jesus to bridge the gap between sinful humanity and himself. Jesus Christ's death on the cross has atoned for our sins (see Rom. 5:8–10; Heb. 10:12). His resurrection justifies us before God the Father (see Rom. 4:25). His ascension guarantees that He intercedes for us at God's right hand (Rom. 8:34). Because of the work of Jesus, God has filled His children with His Spirit, causing our hearts to cry, "Abba, Father!"

when we pray (Gal. 4:6) and giving us the desire to seek Him and honor Him. For those who trust in Jesus and repent of their sins, God the Father is no longer inapproachable—not only are we now able to pray to Him but, in fact, He is the one who invites us to pray. Because of the gracious invitation God issues through the gospel of His Son, prayer is possible.

That's all good news. Our struggle to pray is good, because it reveals that the Spirit has given us a desire to pray. The trouble comes when competing desires distract us from pursuing God. (We also face an enemy who hates it when God's children pray and will do whatever it takes to stop us from engaging in the powerful act.) Sometimes these struggles are because of a lack of head knowledge: *What is prayer about, and why should we do it?* Sometimes they are a heart issue—our sin or pain trips us up. Other times, we simply need to learn practical ways to walk out what we already know.

THE FOUNDATION OF TRUE PRAYER

Let's look at two heart postures that are essential for a true and growing life of prayer.

Faith in God

The number one obstacle to prayer is a lack of faith. James 4:2 says, "You do not have, because you do not ask." And we do not ask because we do not believe—either in God or in prayer. "Without faith it is impossible to please him," writes the author to the Hebrews, "for whoever would draw near to God must believe that he exists and that he rewards those who seek him" (Heb. 11:6). The more we participate in faith-building activities like reading God's Word and fellowshipping with God's people, the easier prayer will become. Prayer is the natural overflow of a growing faith.

Love for God

Not just any type of faith pleases God; even the demons have faith—and shudder (see James 2:19)! True prayer flows from a love for God. When God the Father invites us to Himself through the gospel of His Son, we become His children (see Eph. 1:3–6). As we live in loving obedience to our heavenly Father, we experience more of Him (see John 14:21). And as we experience more of Him, we grow in our love for Him, desire Him more, and, thus, pray more. Because of this, *When Prayer Is a Struggle* is a book about prayer, but it's also a book about the whole Christian life, because we were made to love and worship our Creator, and prayer is one essential expression of devotion to our Lord.

You can't overcome any struggle involving prayer without both *faith in God* and *love for Him*. Faith is the breath in the lungs of the praying life, and love is the heartbeat. We can't move forward on the path of knowing God as we pray without breath in our lungs or blood flowing through our veins. Keep faith and love in mind as we walk through the nine struggles that are presented in this book.

A HEAD-HEART-HANDS APPROACH TO OVERCOMING OBSTACLES

A couple of years ago, my brother Kenny talked me into running an obstacle-course race. The idea was simple: run a 5K and conquer a couple of dozen obstacles along the way. My brother was an accomplished athlete who had won many of these races before; I was a newbie whose primary goal was to not die. He finished the race about an hour before I started mine, which allowed me to pick his brain about the course and hear his advice before running it myself. The wisdom that he shared made the race easier for me and more enjoyable; I avoided rookie mistakes and approached challenging obstacles with the wisdom of a veteran. (I also stayed alive!)

I hope to coach you through obstacles to prayer the way my brother coached me through the obstacles in that race. I'm not a gray-haired sage who has all the answers. I'm a normal guy who realized that he struggled to pray and went on a journey to pursue a more faithful and joyful life of prayer while pleading to God for help along the way. I'm also only one person—and so I've included quotes and stories from other believers, both past and present, to show how they have overcome their struggles and grown in their own love for God.

My driving motivation for writing this book has been the belief that a life of faithful, fruitful, and joyful prayer is within the grasp of every Christian. God has helped me in spectacular ways, and I know that He will help you, too. Do you believe this? If so, will you join me on a journey of thinking long and hard about why we struggle to pray and how we can face our struggles head-on?

Together we will follow a head-heart-hands approach, as we

1. see how gospel truths speak to the struggles we face in prayer (because biblical truth is the solid foundation for faithful prayer);
2. diagnose issues of the heart that keep us from true prayer (because our hearts matter to God); and
3. learn how to move forward in prayer (because informed heads and transformed hearts still need practical help).

I'm a firm believer that you don't learn to pray by reading books any more than you learn to ride a bike by hearing a classroom lecture—you learn by doing.[1] That means if you find

1. I have borrowed this illustration from the Reverend Dick Lucas. See "Interview with Dick Lucas: Your Favorite Preacher's Favorite Preacher," WordPartners, November 30, 2020, https://wordpartners.org/dicklucas.

yourself with the desire to pray while reading this book, set it aside and pray—that's what the book is all about! For this reason, each chapter also includes a prayer and reflection questions.

God can and will change you as you read this book, and that's not because the book is so good—it's because *He* is so good. He is "able to do far more abundantly than all that we ask or think" (Eph. 3:20). Read this book prayerfully. Read it humbly. Read it expectantly. It might surprise you how a little help can take you a long way when God is the one blessing it.

PRAYER

Father God, thank You for calling me to be part of Your family in Jesus. You know my struggles with prayer, my lack of faith, and my lack of love for You and others. Help my unbelief! Increase my love. Cause me to see the world as You do and to see prayer as a gift from Your gracious hand. Convict me of sin and lead me to treasure the cross more greatly. Thank You for all You've done for us by making prayer possible and powerful. In Jesus's name, amen.

QUESTIONS FOR REFLECTION

1. Have you ever felt stuck in your attempts to pray—like a car in the mud with its wheels spinning? If so, why?
2. Explain in your own words why struggling to pray is actually good.
3. Look at this book's table of contents. Which of the nine chapters of the book do you think you need the most? The least?
4. Why are faith and love both crucial for growth in prayer? What would happen if you lacked one or the other?

1

i forget why prayer matters

"I pray because I crave fellowship with my Father. I pray because it shrinks me, my problems, and other people to their proper size. I pray because it's the best way to get the gospel deep into my heart."
—Jack Miller, quoted by Scotty Smith

The late newspaper publisher William Randolph Hearst collected great works of art. One day he heard about some valuable art treasures that he wanted for his collection. So he sent his agent on a search to track down the works. Months passed without success. Then one day the agent finally tracked down information about the owner of the works. After months of waiting, Hearst was surprised to learn that the owner was none other than . . . *William Randolph Hearst!* He had gone to great pains to obtain what he already had access to. He'd forgotten what he already had.[1]

In our spiritual lives, we are often plagued by a similar forgetfulness. So many Christians forget the riches of the gospel that

---

1. Warren W. Wiersbe, *Be Rich: Gaining the Things That Money Can't Buy*, NT Commentary (Ephesians), 2nd ed. (Colorado Springs: David C. Cook, 2009), chap. 3, Kindle.

belong to us in Christ. We long for something that can immediately satisfy, but we forget God and prayer and look for satisfaction in other places. This spiritual forgetfulness opens us up to many spiritual deficiencies.

Before we get too invested in any activity, we first need to understand the *why* behind what we're doing. Business leaders have caught on to this and realize that consumers won't buy in to a product or service unless they understand the *why* behind it.[2] When we don't have clarity about *why* we pray, the *what* (the content of our prayers) and the *how* (the way that we pray) will suffer.

AWESOME NEWS AND FORGETFUL HEARTS

Through our redemption in Christ, we have a direct line to heaven. God never sends His children to voicemail or rejects their calls. And yet none of us pray as we should. We still forget to pray and forget why prayer matters. We wonder whether prayer works. We don't feel like praying unless a trial or major need brings us to our knees, and then once the trial passes or the need is provided for, we go back to our forgetful ways.

Prayer sometimes feels like an annoying item on our to-do lists, similar to paying our bills or flossing our teeth. We are tempted to think about prayer in legalistic terms—as if God's acceptance of us is based solely on the quality or frequency of our prayers. Other times, prayer seems boring and slow in a fast world of noise and entertainment that offers instant gratification. Sometimes it's the hectic pace of our lives that keeps us from prayer.

I'm convinced that every reason behind our inclination to forget the *why* of prayer is the result of one foundational issue:

---

2. See Simon Sinek's teaching in *Start with Why: How Great Leaders Inspire Everyone to Take Action* (New York: Portfolio, 2009) and his TED talk called "How Great Leaders Inspire Action," filmed at Puget Sound, Washington, September [2009], video, 18:34, May 4, 2010, https://www.youtube.com/watch?v=qp0HIF3SfI4.

our lack of faith. As I said in this book's introduction, we can't please God, or truly pray, without faith (see Heb. 11:6). We may think that we are praying, but without faith, the recitation of many words or the mindless mouthing of familiar phrases means nothing to God (see Matt. 6:7).

Now that we've talked about why we forget to pray, let's move on to one of the most important questions that we can ask: Why pray in the first place?

WHY PRAY?

When Jesus taught His disciples to pray through what's known as the Lord's Prayer (see Matt. 6:9–13; Luke 11:2–4),[3] He gave them, and us, the basic grid for *what* we should pray.[4] What we may not realize is that, through this prayer, He also gives us seven reasons for *why* we should pray.

In the English Standard Version's rendition of Matthew 6:9–13, the Lord's Prayer has a mere fifty-two words (fifty-seven in the Greek). If I saw a fifty-two-word review of a product that I was considering buying, I'd probably look for one that was longer and more helpful! And yet these simple words of Jesus provide a comprehensive outlook on both prayer and the Christian life. The late theologian J. I. Packer tells us, "The Lord's Prayer in particular is a marvel of compression, and full of meaning. It is a compendium of the gospel (Tertullian), a body of divinity (Thomas Watson), a rule of purpose as well as of petition, and thus a key to the whole

3. I am indebted to several resources for the material in this section: my pastor, Colin S. Smith's, sermon series "Six Things to Ask of God" (The Orchard Evangelical Free Church, Arlington Heights, IL, May 3–June 7, 2020), available online at unlockingthebible.org/series/six-things-to-ask-of-god/; John Calvin's treatment of the Lord's Prayer in his *Institutes of the Christian Religion*, 3.20.34–49; and J. I. Packer's exposition of it throughout "Learning to Pray: The Lord's Prayer," part 3 within *Growing in Christ* (Wheaton, IL: Crossway, 1994).

4. In chapter 2 we will go into more detail about the content of our prayers.

business of living. What it means to be a Christian is nowhere clearer than here."[5]

We must look at prayer from God's perspective; He's the one to whom we pray, and His perspective is the only one that matters. As we walk through the petitions of the Lord's Prayer, we not only will see God's reasons for why we should pray but will also see a glimpse into the heart He has for the world—and for us. He wants to use this prayer to shape your own heart. Will you let Him?

Pray because God Is Your Father ("Our Father in Heaven")

Prayer is unabashedly God-centered. The first half of the Lord's Prayer focuses on Him, which is a vitally important thing for naturally selfish people in an individualistic age to do. While the second half focuses on our needs, it exalts Him as well—because only a sovereign God could provide what He offers, and only a loving God would offer it in the first place.

The first two words of the Lord's Prayer, "Our Father," indicate *relationship*. One surefire way to get off track during prayer is to forget the nature of this relationship. Some see God as a boss who will be happy with us as long as we put in the spiritual work of praying and see results. (You might call this a contractual approach to prayer.) Others see him as an ATM or Santa Claus–like figure who will automatically give us what we want without having any interest in a real relationship. Or perhaps God is like the Force in Star Wars, and prayer to this impersonal "force" is nothing more than throwing wishful thinking into the air and

5. Packer, *Growing in Christ*, 136. I appreciate the words of Martin Luther found in *A Simple Way to Pray*, trans. Matthew C. Harrison (St. Louis: Concordia Publishing House, 2012), 15, as well: "To this day, I nurse on the Lord's Prayer like a little child, and as an old man now, I eat and drink from it, but never get my fill." I'll throw in another illustration: the Lord's Prayer can simultaneously serve as a kiddie pool for learning the basics of prayer while also having a deep end that is so profound that the most mature believers will never plumb its depth.

hoping that the winds of the universe blow in our direction. But for those who are in Christ, God is Father.

If there's one thing that I want every reader of this book to take away with them, it's that God loves you unconditionally as a *Father*. Before we had saving faith in Christ, Scripture says we were enemies of God (see Rom. 5:6–10), dead in sin (see Eph. 2:1), sons of disobedience (see Eph. 2:2), and children of wrath (see Eph. 2:3). The glorious truth of the gospel is that despite our wickedness and opposition to God, He sent His Son to the cross for sinners like us (see Rom. 5:8) and now adopts us into His family as beloved children. He fills us with His Spirit to testify of His love for us (see Rom. 5:5) and to enable us to cry "Abba! Father!" to Him in prayer (see Rom. 8:15–16). A good earthly father cares for his children, wants them to come to him when they're in pain, and wants to provide for their every need. How much more does our perfect Father in heaven care for us and want to hear from us—His beloved children!

I recently met a Christian woman from Ireland and heard her testimony. For many years she lived as a content unbeliever who had dabbled in religion in the past. A friend invited her to a Bible study, and she decided to go. "I had no idea what was going on when they studied the Bible. But when they prayed—*oh, how they prayed!*—they prayed like they actually knew God! And that told me I needed what they had." She recognized that a real relationship with God the Father is possible and that it is oh, so good.

When you pray the Lord's Prayer, don't skip past "Our Father." Dwell on God's character and His relationship with you. Remember His redemptive work throughout human history. Rejoice in His extravagant grace—because "to grasp [God as Father] is to know oneself rich and privileged beyond any monarch or millionaire."[6]

---

6. Packer, *Growing in Christ*, 146.

Pray because You Want His Name to Be Praised ("Hallowed Be Your Name")

To *hallow* means to treat as holy, to revere, to sanctify. Hallowing God's name means not taking it lightly. God loves the glory of His name enough to build the honoring of it into the Ten Commandments: "You shall not take the name of the LORD your God in vain" (Ex. 20:7). The root of the Hebrew word for *vain* connotes "emptiness" or "nothingness."[7] Using God's name in an empty way doesn't convey the honor and glory that He is due.

Heaven is the gold standard for demonstrating the proper way God's name is to be exalted. The book of Revelation repeatedly pulls back the curtain to reveal how God's name is exalted in the heavenly worship of angels and saints. Here's one example.

> Great and amazing are your deeds,
>> O Lord God the Almighty!
> Just and true are your ways,
>> O King of the nations!
> Who will not fear, O Lord,
>> and glorify your name?
> For you alone are holy.
>> All nations will come
>> and worship you,
> for your righteous acts have been revealed. (Rev. 15:3–4)[8]

Unfortunately, our world falls far short of heaven's standard. God's name is used as a cuss word or a punchline and is even openly mocked. "The name of God is blasphemed among the Gentiles," writes Paul in Romans 2:24, in reference to the prophet Isaiah. And yet it's not just the Gentiles who blaspheme God's name; Paul's next

---

7. *The Enhanced Brown-Driver-Briggs Hebrew and English Lexicon*, ed. Francis Brown with S. R. Driver and Charles A. Briggs (Oxford: Clarendon Press, 1977), s.v. "שָׁוְא."
8. See also Revelation 4:8–11; 5:9–14; 7:9–12; 11:17–19; 16:5–6; 19:1–9.

words, "*because of you*," indicate that even God's people can dishonor His holy name by living sinful lives. That's why Jesus wants us to start our prayers with worship, by saying "Hallowed be Your name."

When we pray, "Hallowed be Your name," we ask for God to exalt His name in all the earth. We ask for all people to honor and glorify His name. And we ask for His help to live in a way that honors Him. We ask Him to help us to glorify Him in all we do (see 1 Cor. 10:31). He is worthy!

Pray because You Want His Kingly Rule to Expand ("Your Kingdom Come")

Several years ago, while on a trip in order to train pastors in Latin America, I sat in a pastor's office in one of Ecuador's largest cities while preparing my heart to preach in thirty minutes' time. Pastor Jaime offered me coffee and started sharing the history of his church's building. I was a little confused at first (I don't normally enjoy hearing anecdotes of foreign real-estate transactions before I preach), but soon Jaime's story gripped me.

Jaime and his wife Lirio had been grieving the destructive impact that a local nightclub was making on their community: local youth were being led astray, households were being destroyed, and crime rates were increasing. So Jaime and Lirio began to pray for the nightclub to close. They continued to pray for about five years—until one day, by God's grace, it closed. The building where it had been sat empty for two years.

Meanwhile, God was reaching people through the church that Jaime was pastoring, so the church sent Jaime and his family to plant a new branch of the congregation. But where would it meet? Jaime and his church family prayed for a location that would help him to reach more people with the gospel. And the best option turned out to be the former nightclub that was sitting empty. After discussing the opportunity with the building's owner and sharing the gospel with him, Jaime bought the building for half the asking price. Now the church meets in the former night-club—proclaiming the gospel in the community, strengthening families, and reaching youth in the process. Crime in the area even went down. God turned a den of darkness into an embassy for Christ's kingdom. By praying for the closure of the nightclub and for the gospel to be advanced through their ministry, Jaime and Lirio were praying for God's kingdom to come.

God is working all throughout human history to build a people for Himself. While even the greatest nations on earth come and go, God's kingdom is eternal. While earthly nations have fixed borders, God's kingdom encompasses people from every tribe, tongue, and nation. Jesus is building His church, and the gates of hell won't prevail against it (see Matt. 16:18). That is true whether you're in Quito, Quebec, or Queensland.

To pray "Your kingdom come" is to express our longing for God's perfect rule on earth. It is to bow before King Jesus and forsake our personal kingdoms. It is to acknowledge the transience of earthly kingdoms and their true place in history (see Ps. 2; Dan. 2). It is to ask for God to bring salvation to the lost and judgment to His enemies. With these words, we pray that He will cripple the domain of darkness and speed ahead the advance of the kingdom of light. We ask Him to help us to live with His kingdom in mind as we raise our kids and talk to our neighbors.

Praying "Your kingdom come" also helps us to look ahead to the ultimate ushering in of His kingdom—one that is closer to you than when you first started reading this chapter—when "the dwelling place of God [will be] with man" and when "He will wipe away every tear from [our] eyes" (Rev. 21:3–4). Come, Lord Jesus!

Pray because You Want His Perfect Will to Be Done ("Your Will Be Done, on Earth as It Is in Heaven")

I still remember when I heard the news—Mom had cancer and needed immediate surgery. But a successful surgery didn't fully take the cancer away. Our family prayed for healing and persevered with my mom, for three and a half years, through chemo treatments, hospital visits, encouraging prognoses, and discouraging ones, while shedding many tears along the way. When the outlook was bleak, we prayed for more time, and God mercifully granted her the health to attend my wedding as well as my brother's five weeks later. But on March 22, 2016, with our whole family huddled around her bed, Denise Halloran breathed her last. Moments after we saw my mom pass into the Lord's presence, my dad quoted Job 1:21: "The LORD gave, and the LORD has taken away; blessed be the name of the LORD."

God wants us to pray "Your will be done," as Christ did in the garden (Matt. 26:42), to help us to acknowledge that His ways, wisdom, and purposes are higher than ours. To remind ourselves of our creatureliness and His omnipotence. To humble ourselves.

When we don't pray in a posture that says "Your will be done," we are shaking our fists at God and saying, "My will is better!" Such pride makes prayers ineffective, for "God opposes the proud but gives grace to the humble" (James 4:6). That's not to say that we can't wrestle with God in prayer, but at the end of the day we must humbly submit to our Maker out of confidence in His good and eternal purposes for us (see Rom. 8:28–29). Only when we submit to God's will can we worship while in tremendous pain.

"Prayer is surrender," writes E. Stanley Jones—"surrender to the will of God and cooperation with that will. If I throw out a boathook from the boat and catch hold of the shore and pull, do I pull the shore to me, or do I pull myself to the shore? Prayer is not pulling God to my will, but the aligning of my will to the will of God."[9] Sometimes our most genuine worship comes in the

---

9. E. Stanley Jones, *A Song of Ascents* (Nashville: Abingdon, 1968), 383, quoted in Kent Hughes and Barbara Hughes, *Liberating Ministry from The Success Syndrome* (Wheaton, IL: Tyndale House, 1988), 73.

wake of bad news, when we can say from the depths of our hearts, "Blessed be the name of the Lord" and "Your will be done."

Pray because You Need His Provision ("Give Us This Day Our Daily Bread")

Because "the earth is the LORD's, and everything in it" (Ps. 24:1 NIV), we can confidently ask our omnipotent Creator to meet our needs—He owns it all anyway! When we ask for His provision of any need we have (bread, a job, finances, wisdom, encouragement, faith, strength to endure persecution, safety, or guidance for a life situation), we acknowledge His power to provide as well as our reliance on Him. When we recite this petition from the Lord's Prayer and think of all that He has provided throughout the decades of our lives, we grow grateful to our Provider. When we pray for our daily bread, we also expand our horizons by being led to think of others in need and how God may want to use us to provide for *them.*

Although this petition focuses on our temporal needs, it also reminds us of God's greater spiritual provision. Yes, we need physical bread and other material goods. But at a more foundational level, we need spiritual bread. "I am the bread of life," Jesus said. "Whoever comes to me shall not hunger, and whoever believes in me shall never thirst" (John 6:35). Elsewhere, He said that "man shall not live by bread alone, but by every word that comes from the mouth of God" (Matt. 4:4; see also Deut. 8:3). Our spiritual appetite is satisfied only by God's Word, written and incarnate.

We have great needs in this world—both physical and spiritual. And our great God and King "will supply every need of yours according to his riches in glory in Christ Jesus" (Phil. 4:19). God's provision won't always look the way we expect or come according to our timing, but we can be confident that He wouldn't teach us to pray for provision if He weren't willing and able to provide exactly what we needed.

Pray because You Need His Forgiveness ("Forgive Us Our Debts, as We Also Have Forgiven Our Debtors")

This next petition reminds us how important relationships are to God. We need God's forgiveness when we sin, and we need to extend forgiveness to others when they sin against us. If we didn't do this, how could we follow the first and second Great Commandments—to love God and love our neighbors (see Matt. 22:37–40)?

We first ask God to forgive us our "debts," which we incur when we come up short in fulfilling our duty, and which are known simply as sin (see the wording of the parallel passage in Luke 11:4). While believers can rest confidently because Christ has paid for their sins on the cross (see Rom. 8:1), our sin grieves the Holy Spirit of God (see Eph. 4:30) and thus hinders our ability to commune with God through the Spirit. When we ask Him for pardon, we acknowledge our sinfulness—as well as our inability to do anything about it on our own. Our only hope is to issue a desperate cry for help, from a broken heart, to a faithful Father who hears. His loving heart is moved to forgive, because the sufficiency of Christ's sacrifice on the cross covers our sin and makes forgiveness possible.

Tying our forgiveness (by saying "forgive us our debts") with the forgiveness we grant to others (when we say "as we also have forgiven our debtors") reminds us that *forgiven people forgive* (see Matt. 18:21–35; Eph. 4:32). Other people let us down in many ways and don't pay us what they owe—be it respect, time, energy, or something else. But we can't let their failure prohibit us from loving them as God desires. If we do, the weeds of bitterness, anger, jealousy, and hatred grow in our hearts. God wants His children to walk in love with Him and with one another. Our past sin hinders this, and that's why the next petition requests protection from future sin.

Pray because You Need His Deliverance ("Lead Us Not into Temptation, but Deliver Us from Evil")

After God signs our adoption papers and welcomes us to His family, He signs our enlistment papers for a spiritual battle. It's a battle that we've been in since birth, but we don't see it until the Spirit opens our eyes.

"Lead us not into temptation" is a plea for God's help with fighting our internal battle against "the passions of the flesh, which wage war against your soul" (1 Peter 2:11). This petition acknowledges the weakness of our flesh and our willpower in the face of temptation. It's a reminder that sin is deceptive and that our only hope is to "be strong *in the Lord* and in the strength of *his* might" (Eph. 6:10). As I've grown older, I've seen horrible sin crop up in many people's lives where you would least expect it, making me realize how weak and vulnerable we all are. "Let anyone who thinks that he stands take heed lest he fall," warns the apostle Paul (1 Cor. 10:12). Praying for God's help reminds us that He won't let us be tempted beyond what we can endure and that He promises a way of escape (see 1 Cor. 10:13).

Praying "Deliver us from evil" reminds us of the battle that we also fight with an external enemy. Some translations say, "Deliver us from *the evil one*"—referring to Satan. Satan hates God's people and their prayers, and he will do whatever he can to keep us from praying.[10] When we pray for deliverance from evil, we acknowledge God's power to deliver us due to His supremacy over every spiritual being (see Eph. 1:20–21; Col. 1:16). We express our desire for "increases of God's grace [to] continually be showered upon us, until, completely filled therewith, we triumph over all evil."[11] We

10. As the old hymn says, "Satan trembles when he sees the weakest saint upon his knees." William Cowper, "What Various Hindrances We Meet," 1779.

11. *Calvin: Institutes of the Christian Religion*, vol. 2, *Books III.XX to IV.XX*, ed. John T. McNeill, trans. Ford Lewis Battles (Philadelphia: The Westminster Press, 1960), 3.20.46.

need God's deliverance from evil spiritual powers and from human pawns of the enemy that seek to devour us as a lion does its prey (see 1 Peter 5:8). Prayers for deliverance from enemies pervade the Psalms (see Pss. 35; 59; 140; 143), and the apostle Paul repeatedly asked even fellow believers to pray for him to be delivered from his human enemies (see Rom. 15:30–33; 2 Cor. 1:8–11; 2 Thess. 3:1–5). Why should we think we're immune?

REMEMBERING WHY PRAYER MATTERS

We pray in order to glorify God. We pray in order to unify our hearts with His kingdom vision for the world and to align ourselves with His will. We pray for provision, restored relationships, and protection from the evil that comes from both inside us and outside.

If you sometimes realize that you've gone for almost a whole day (or for several days) without even thinking of God or prayer, take heart. I've been there too, and many other believers have as well. But you can't stay there. Don't forget that prayer flows from faith—and because of that, perhaps the most effective action to take in order to remember the purpose of prayer is to pray for faith that will go on to express itself in prayer.

How might you grow your faith? How might you remind yourself of the importance of prayer? I try to keep reminders always before me: a sticky note on the bathroom mirror, framed art containing the Lord's Prayer in my kitchen, a daily phone notification that asks me if it's "Time to Pray." I try as best as I can to build prayer into my relationships, for a little added accountability, as well as into my routines, so that it becomes a habit. As I fellowship regularly with the church, prayer becomes more natural.

As with all the struggles that we'll examine in this book, the key to growth in this area is not immediate perfection; it is making small and faithful progress while remaining confident in who God is and in the gracious invitation He has offered us to pray. You will still lack faith. You will still sometimes forget why prayer matters. But over time you will better remember the *why* of prayer.

In the next chapter, we'll look more closely at what the content of our prayers should be.

PRAYER

Dear heavenly Father, thank You for adopting me into Your family and giving Your Son for me. Thank You for the glorious and undeserved invitation you have offered me to come into Your presence through prayer. I admit that I often forget to pray and that, deep down, I lack faith. Stir in me a heart of prayer, by Your Spirit, and help me to grow as a person of humble, moment-by-moment dependence on You. Please use this little book to show me how I can experience more of Your grandeur and glory through prayer. In Jesus's name, amen.

QUESTIONS FOR REFLECTION

1. What has most helped you to grow in prayer?
2. Are you ever tempted to view God as a boss, an ATM, or an impersonal force like in Star Wars? How should viewing God as Father change your perspective?
3. Of the seven reasons to pray that the Lord's Prayer gives us, which one do you need to focus on the most?
4. What changes can you make in your life to help you better remember God's invitation to pray?

2

i don't know what to pray

"You may think your prayers are nothing to write home about. That's fine. You are not writing home, but heaven. God is merciful. He accepts your lame prayers. What he wants is not your eloquence but your heart." —Jared C. Wilson, The Pastor's Justification

I love hiking. There's nothing like breathing in fresh air, getting exercise, and enjoying the great outdoors with friends and family. And while I'm not too picky about where I hike, I do have one nonnegotiable: there has to be a path. You'd have to be crazy to pull off on the side of the road and bushwhack your way through dense brush. I have no interest in twisting my ankle in a hole, hurdling fallen trees, getting lost, or finding myself cornered by a hungry animal. (Maybe I'm just not adventurous?)

And yet, when many Christians approach God in prayer, they don't choose a path for doing so—and thus they soon find themselves running out of words or else praying the same ones over and over. Discouraged by these setbacks, they settle for less or give up completely. But it doesn't have to be this way.

This chapter will help us to know what the *content* of our

prayers should be.[1] It will help with personal prayer as well as group prayer. While I can't be comprehensive in this chapter, I can provide a framework for how we can approach prayer along with several paths for us to walk down. A clear path gives our minds direction and our hearts the freedom to express themselves. Think of a path for prayer like a wooden trellis that allows the vine of prayer to extend itself and grow. Without a trellis, a vine would not be able to extend itself—it would clump up on the ground and even die. Often the same thing happens with our prayers if we don't give them a path to follow.

Before we dig in to the meat of this chapter, I'll let you in on a secret: when you are done with it, you will realize that prayer is easier and more effective than you ever imagined.

WE NEED SCRIPTURE
TO SHAPE OUR PRAYERS

Prayer is a journey to God's heart for the purpose of knowing Him, pleading His help, and conforming ourselves to His will. It is a response to the Word He has spoken to us. The only way we can know Him, His character, and His will is through His revealed Word—the Bible.

The Word of God needs to shape and fill our prayers, for a few reasons. First, it allows us to prioritize God's holy desires for us instead of relying on our own finite minds, our fleshly impulses, or other influences. "The richness of the Word of God ought to determine our prayer, not the poverty of our heart," wrote Dietrich Bonhoeffer.[2] Second, since we also want prayer to be *effective*, God is more likely to work through our prayers when

---

1. Chapter 7 will help us to know how to organize this content and form our requests into daily, weekly, and monthly rhythms of prayer.
2. Dietrich Bonhoeffer, *Psalms: The Prayer Book of the Bible* (repr., Philadelphia: Fortress Press, 1974), 15.

we pray in accordance with His truth. "And this is the confidence that we have toward him," writes John the apostle, "that if we ask anything according to his will he hears us" (1 John 5:14). John Piper describes this principle in another way: "There is a direct connection between the degree to which our minds are shaped by Scripture and the degree to which our prayers are answered."[3]

FIVE PATHS TO TAKE WHEN WE PRAY

Now that we understand why the Bible needs to inform and drive our prayers, let's look at five paths to take when we pray.

Path #1: Learn to Pray from Scriptural Prayers

All Scripture is useful for growing in prayer, but there is extra value in learning from the prayers it contains—all of which the Holy Spirit inspired (see 2 Peter 1:20–21). The biblical record, from Genesis to Revelation, is peppered with prayers from Jesus, Moses, the prophets, the apostles, and many others. What did they pray for? How did God respond? How can we learn from the content of their prayers and from their examples? When you read the Bible, look for prayers that you can incorporate into your own prayer life.[4] And while you can find many such prayers throughout Scripture, there are two uniquely valuable places to turn.

The Psalms. Psalms is the only book in Scripture that is 100 percent comprised of prayers. It is a treasure trove of theology-laden, emotion-driven songs of praise. Written by David, Solomon, the sons of Korah, Moses, Asaph, and others, the psalms offer prayers for every situation and emotion imaginable—from the deep pain of lament found in Psalm 88 to the joyful worship of Psalm 150,

3. John Piper, "Tips for Praying the Word," Desiring God, January 9, 1984, https://www.desiringgod.org/articles/tips-for-praying-the-word.

4. I'll share in chapter 7 how we can work specific prayers into our routines.

and everything in between. They give us words for when our hearts fail us, and they serve as the emotional soundtrack of God's worshipping people.

While they were originally given to Israel, the psalms have special importance for the Christian. Like the rest of the Old Testament, they point us to Jesus and find their true fulfillment only in Him (see Luke 24:44). Jesus, the true Israelite, embodied Israel's hymnbook more than anyone else in history. The Savior's life was so shaped by the psalms that He quoted them in His dying breaths. The psalms also had special importance for Christ's apostles, who prayed and quoted them often. The apostle Paul wrote that saturating our minds and relationships with the Psalms helps the Word of Christ to dwell in us richly (see Col. 3:16) and the Spirit to fill our lives (see Eph. 5:18–19).

There is no one right way of using the Psalms in your prayers. The most straightforward way is to pray a psalm verbatim. One pastor recommends two more ways that you can use the Psalms to pray: "You can either take the pleas and praises of the Psalms as your own, picking them like apples. Or you can decorate the psalm like a Christmas tree, hanging your pleas and praises on it."[5] In addition to giving shape to your prayers, reading the prayer of a psalmist may jump-start your heart for prayer and change "your vocabulary, your language, your attitude."[6]

I'll admit that the psalms sometimes make me uncomfortable. They push me outside my comfort zone and give vent to emotions that I'm used to holding back. Yet they also make me feel certain emotions and see life through the experience of the psalmist. Ultimately, they lead me to trust in God during life's

5. Benjamin Kandt, "How to Pray the Psalms," PrayPsalms.org, July 16, 2017, https://praypsalms.org/how-to-pray-the-psalms-60484747091a.

6. Tim Keller, "How to Pray the Psalms," interview on *Ask Pastor John*, no. 459, Desiring God, October 27, 2014, https://www.desiringgod.org/interviews/how-to-pray-the-psalms.

peaks and valleys. Flip to the appendix to see suggested Psalms that you can pray in various situations.

The prayers of the apostle Paul. Scattered throughout his thirteen epistles are many prayers by the apostle Paul—some long and glorious, others short and sweet. I consider Paul's prayers to be a broad category—one that includes both his actual prayers and the glimpses he gives into his prayer life. These glimpses allow us to see things such as Paul's reasons for thanksgiving, his reports on personal prayers, his requests for prayer, and his benedictions.[7] These prayers and glimpses reveal the heart Paul has for God and his Spirit-inspired priorities. Themes that dominate Paul's prayers include spiritual growth, living according to God's will, spiritual strength, the spread of the gospel, and thankfulness for God's work in the lives of believers. His emphasis on these things helps us to remember what is of first importance—the gospel (see 1 Cor. 15:3)—and the fact that we should prioritize spiritual growth and gospel fruit over our smaller, more temporal needs (although God cares about those, too!).

Before we move on to the next path, I encourage you to make the prayer of Romans 15:13 your own at this very moment: "May the God of hope fill you with all joy and peace in believing, so that by the power of the Holy Spirit you may abound in hope."

Path #2: Pray as You Read the Bible

It's easiest to get into a conversation when someone speaks to us first. God speaks to us in His Word; and if we pray with an

---

7. See the appendix for a list of prayers from Paul that I recommend studying. To get deeper into Paul and his prayers, consider reading D. A. Carson's *Praying with Paul: A Call to Spiritual Reformation* (Grand Rapids: Baker Academic, 2015) or Charles Spurgeon's *Lessons from the Apostle Paul's Prayers* (n.p.: Cross-Points, 2018). You can also find a complete compilation of his prayers in PDF form at Kevin Halloran, "A Complete List of the Apostle Paul's Prayers in the Bible," *Anchored in Christ* (blog), February 8, 2014, https://www.kevinhalloran.net/the-apostle-pauls-prayers-in-the-bible/.

open Bible, we don't need to think of words to pray to Him. We can simply respond to what He has said.

While praying Scripture doesn't require a specific method, I recommend the 3-R method,[8] which you can use with any of the Bible's 1,189 chapters.[9]

To pray using this method, first read a portion of Scripture and ask for God's help with understanding His Word.[10] Then recognize what God wants to communicate through the passage. Whether you read a single verse, an entire book of the Bible, or something in between, ponder how God wants to communicate

- a characteristic of Himself to behold
- a truth to believe
- a sin to fight
- a command to obey
- an example to learn from

Consider the overarching ideas of a passage, because they will usually harmonize smaller ideas and cause you to pray about

8. This method comes directly from the way Ben Patterson recommends praying through the Psalms in *God's Prayer Book: The Power and Pleasure of Praying the Psalms* (Carol Stream, IL: Tyndale Momentum, 2008), 20. Pastor and author Kevin DeYoung recommends Patterson's approach and has said, "This simple tool has helped me pray the Bible more than any other single strategy. I've used [it] in my devotional times and have employed it often in leading others in prayer." Kevin DeYoung, "How to Pray Using Scripture," *DeYoung, Restless, and Reformed* (blog), The Gospel Coalition, January 4, 2013, https://www.thegospelcoalition.org/blogs/kevin-deyoung/how-to-pray-using-scripture/.

9. Some portions of Scripture will be easier to pray than others. If you're looking for good ones to start with, I find John Piper's recommendation helpful: "[Pray] ethical portions of Scripture like Matthew 5–7; Romans 12; 1 Corinthians 13; Galatians 5–6; Ephesians 4–6; Colossians 3–4; 1 Thessalonians 5; 1 John, etc." John Piper, "How to Pray for Half-an-Hour," Desiring God, January 5, 1982, https://www.desiringgod.org/articles/how-to-pray-for-half-an-hour.

10. I often begin my Bible reading by praying two verses from Psalm 119: "Open my eyes, that I may behold wondrous things out of your law" (v. 18) and "Turn my eyes from looking at worthless things; and give me life in your ways" (v. 37). I like these verses so much that I have them on a Post-it note inside the cover of my Bible.

something of greater importance. And don't let a lack of confidence in the way you read the Bible intimidate you. You may misinterpret it or make mistakes. Trust, though, that the God of the Scriptures will keep you anchored far closer to His heart than if you are left to your own devices when you pray.

Once you have read a passage in this way, you are ready to pray the three Rs.

1. Rejoice. When the passage you are reading reveals something about God, His character, or the truth of His universe, rejoice in it! We can rejoice in any passage of Scripture, because God and the gospel of His Son are that good (see Phil. 4:4)!

2. Repent. How does the passage show you that you have fallen short of God's standard? Confess your sins—and acknowledge His glorious grace, which invites you to confess and to receive cleansing (see Ps. 32; 1 John 1:9).

3. Request. In what areas do you need to ask God's help, for yourself or for others, so that they can better obey what the passage teaches? Bring your requests before our Sovereign King.

The 3-R method gives us three simple prompts for turning Scripture into prayer, thereby fostering a proper response to God's Word. As we grow in our understanding of His Word, through personal study and church participation, this method will prove more and more useful for both personal and public prayers.

Path #3: Follow the Lord's Prayer

In the last chapter we looked at why we should pray, and we turned to Jesus, who taught His disciples to pray through what is known as "the Lord's Prayer." And not only does this prayer show us why we should pray, as we have seen, it also tells us *what* we should pray for—which makes it the perfect template for us to use for prayers of our own.

You might take a *general* approach and pray petition by petition, filling in specific praises and requests as you go. Starting with "Hallowed be Your name," for instance, you might praise God for His character, His glory that is displayed in creation, and His work in your life and in your church. You can stay on this petition for as long as you want, or until you can't think of anything else to pray for, and then move to the next—repeating the process until you finish the prayer. Praying our way through each petition of the Lord's Prayer like this gives us a well-rounded and focused session of praying. Martin Luther employed this method, and recommended the technique to others, in his little book *A Simple Way to Pray*. I've found this method to be a helpful way of focusing my mind for prayer and even reengaging it when my prayer time gets interrupted: *I just left off with "Your will be done"; now on to "Give us this day our daily bread"!*

I also use a *specific* approach and apply the whole of the Lord's Prayer to one person or situation at a time. I've found this to be a helpful way to pray for both spiritual battles and everyday matters. Here's an example of how I use this approach to pray for my marriage.

- *Our Father in heaven, hallowed be Your name*—in our marriage, our life together, our interactions, and our witness to the world.
- *Your kingdom come*, in and through our marriage. Would we bow the knee to Your kingship more willingly, and would our witness cause others to love Jesus and to desire Your kingdom.
- *Your will be done*, in the life we live together. We have dreams and desires, but we lay them at Your feet. Guide

us according to Your perfect will so that You may receive maximal glory through us.

- *Give us this day our daily bread*—finances to pay the bills and the health to live faithfully. Thank You for the abundant blessings You have given us. Show us how we can be Your hands and feet by providing for the needs of others.
- *Forgive us our debts*—Lord, You know that we need forgiveness. We sin and respond sinfully to each other's sin. We need Your forgiveness—as well as Your strength so that we can extend forgiveness to each other and to others in our lives.
- *Lead us not into temptation*—Father, there are so many sins we could commit that could destroy our marriage and hurt the trust that we have in each other. Please kill the tiny sins in our hearts and strengthen our resolve to follow Your Word in holiness. Deliver our marriage and our household from evil so that we may we be a beacon of light for You on our block, at our church, and in our world.

Jesus taught His disciples to pray using the Lord's Prayer, and the wise will do just that. How can you use the Lord's Prayer as a template for the way you pray about your relationships, responsibilities, community, and anxieties?

Path #4: Follow the ACTS Pattern

The ACTS prayer structure has helped believers for generations. ACTS stands for *adoration, confession, thanksgiving,* and *supplication.* Listing these four types of prayer in this particular order makes ACTS a useful tool for approaching God.

Adoration. This first type sets the tone for prayer, as the Lord's Prayer does, by setting our hearts on God's character and works. While we have access to God and can be bold because of Jesus's work, we should not just rush to make demands of Him when we pray. God created us to worship Him (see Isa. 43:7), and we should pray as worshippers. R.C. Sproul said this about beginning prayer with adoration: "I've noticed over many years that as we grow in the discipline and in the delight of prayer, it seems that we naturally spend more and more of our time on this first element."[11]

Confession. In confession, you acknowledge your guilt before God. When you confess, be specific about admitting both sinful outward actions and inward attitudes. Admit that you have not loved Him or others as you should. Confess specific sins—and ask Him to convict you of others of which you are unaware.

Thanksgiving. In thanksgiving, you express gratitude to God for what He has given you. If you are in Jesus, then you can always thank Him for salvation, for loving you as His beloved child, and for His continual presence in your life. Thank Him, as well, for His daily provision and the grace He shows in a thousand forms.

Supplication. This fourth type of prayer presents our needs, the needs of others, and other requests before God.

As a less mature believer, I would jump through the hoops of A, C, and T as quickly as I could, in order to get to S, and then I'd back up a dump truck of requests and unload them. Don't be like me. The main person who I shortchanged was myself. We don't want to treat God like a wish-granting genie; we want to grow in our faith in Him and the love we have for Him as our Father. We want to submit ourselves to Him and to His good purposes, and we want prayer to change us—not only our outward circumstances. Adoring God, confessing our sins, and thanking

11. R.C. Sproul, *The Prayer of the Lord* (Orlando: Reformation Trust Publishing, 2018), chap. 6, Kindle.

Him might seem like eating our vegetables at first. But, just like eating vegetables, including these elements in our prayer gives us the spiritual nutrients we need in order to live vibrant and spiritually healthy lives.

Path #5: Pray Written Prayers

I used to think that reading the prayers of others didn't count as prayer in the eyes of God. I mean, isn't that like copying answers during a test? But then I realized that the songs we sing to God from our hearts, each Sunday, have been written by someone else; why would praying a prayer written by someone else be any less honoring to Him if we mean what we're praying?

Many saints, in both the past and the present, have recorded heartfelt and biblically rooted prayers that stir our affections and lift our hearts heavenward. For my specific recommendations, see the recommended resources at the back of the book.

I hope you will find one or more of these five paths to take during prayer to have a transformational effect on your walk with God. Now, before we finish this chapter, let's look at three more ways God has given us to help us to find words to pray.

PRAYER AS A TEAM SPORT

As children, we learn to talk by hearing others speak. Similarly, we learn to pray by hearing others speak to God. "Plain and simple," writes Pastor David Mathis, "the best way to learn to pray is pray with others who have had their prayers shaped by the Scriptures."[12] This community nature of prayer shouldn't be a surprise. After all, Jesus taught His disciples not to pray "*My* Father in heaven" but to pray "*Our* Father in heaven"!

12. David Mathis, *Habits of Grace: Enjoying Jesus through the Spiritual Disciplines* (Wheaton, IL: Crossway, 2016), 115.

Opportunities for us to grow by listening to the prayers of others abound. Pastoral prayers during worship services teach us how to pray. So do prayer meetings and small groups. It's beautiful to hear other sons and daughters of God cry out to Him for the salvation of loved ones, for the spread of the gospel in our surrounding community, and for the members of our church to grow in faith and love. "The local church serves as a greenhouse where our prayers thrive,"[13] writes John Onwuchekwa.

A pastor at our church repeatedly encouraged one woman in her sixties to attend a monthly prayer meeting. She politely declined invitation after invitation. Then, one day, she went. It changed her. "I'd never gone to a prayer meeting, but now I won't miss one," the woman shared with the pastor after attending it. "It was so encouraging to hear other believers pray to their Father."

The prayers of others often minister to me and shape my own prayers. My friend Ryan often prays, in our men's early-morning small group, "Lord, we don't deserve the good gift of coffee or the opportunity to meet together." My colleague David often draws from the words of Philippians 2:3–4 in his prayers: "God, help us consider others as more important than ourselves." And my friend Juan from Ecuador reminds me of God's nearness by approaching God as "Papito Dios"—his Spanish adaptation of the New Testament's "Abba, Father" language.

Praying with the church isn't only for the purpose of teaching one another to pray by example. We experience more of God, and our prayers enjoy a special power, as we fellowship together (see Matt. 18:19–20; James 5:14–16).[14] We are the body of Christ—living stones being built into a spiritual house where God's Spirit

---

13. John Onwuchekwa, *Prayer: How Praying Together Shapes the Church* (Wheaton, IL: Crossway, 2018), 62.

14. I love how J. I. Packer said it: "Christian fellowship . . . is not an end in itself. Fellowship between Christians is for the sake of fellowship with God." Quote from *God's Words: Studies of Key Bible Themes* (Grand Rapids: Baker Book House, 1981), 194.

dwells (see Eph. 2:19–22; 1 Peter 2:5). Just as stones grow in value when they are part of a house, the unified voice of the body of Christ is greater than the sum of its parts.

THE SECRET TO WARMING UP
YOUR HEART FOR PRAYER

Even with the aforementioned paths for seeking God in prayer as well as the example of others, we sometimes don't desire to pray. Our hearts are cold and need a jump start. Puritan Thomas Watson offers the diagnosis and the remedy: "The reason we come away so cold from reading the word is, because we do not warm ourselves at the fires of meditation."[15]

Meditating on Scripture is simply turning a passage over and over in your mind the way a jeweler rotates a diamond to showcase its various facets. As our concentration on this Scripture deepens, our hearts warm to its truths and prayer becomes natural. This is why some have called meditation a bridge between Bible reading and prayer.[16] We start in the Bible and dwell on its rich truths, and those truths move us to pray. J. I. Packer and Carolyn Nystrom describe what happens: "Thinking in the presence of God becomes talking to the Lord directly, and talking to God leads back to further thinking in his presence. This is a natural transition, both ways."[17]

Like someone walking back and forth across a bridge, we

15. Thomas Watson, "How We May Read the Scriptures with Most Spiritual Profit," in *Puritan Sermons: 1659–1689* (Wheaton, IL: Richard Owen Roberts Publishing, 1981), 2:62, quoted in Donald S. Whitney, *Spiritual Disciplines for the Christian Life*, rev. and updated ed. (Colorado Springs: NavPress, 2014), 50, quoted in David Mathis, "Warm Yourself at the Fires of Meditation," Desiring God, March 26, 2014, https://www.desiringgod.org/articles/warm-yourself-at-the-fires-of-meditation.

16. See Timothy Keller, *Prayer: Experiencing Awe and Intimacy with God* (2014; repr., New York: Penguin Books, 2016), 90.

17. J. I. Packer and Carolyn Nystrom, *Praying: Finding Our Way Through Duty to Delight* (2006; repr., Downers Grove, IL: IVP Books, 2009), 75.

may move from Bible reading to prayer and back again as we meditate. We hear from God and His Word, and we respond in prayer. We give Him time and hearts that are available for His Spirit to teach us His Word, and He does so. His Word plunges into the depths of our souls, and he changes our minds, our hearts, and our wills.

WHEN THE STRUGGLES OF LIFE LEAVE US SPEECHLESS

You've seen several pathways for approaching God in prayer, as well as how learning from others and meditating on God's Word can also help us, in this chapter, which means that the excuse "I don't know what to say when I'm praying" isn't valid—*most of the time*. Some of the time, however, "we do not know what to pray for as we ought" (Rom. 8:26), and it's not because of ignorance; it's due to the trials and tribulations of living in a fallen world. If you've ever tried to pray during great suffering, then you are familiar with this experience. You know that you *should* pray, but your heart feels numb. Your trial has knocked the wind out of you, and you can't focus long enough to squeak out more than a word or two. All that you can offer God is the groan that the rest of creation offers as it longs for rescue from the suffering of life (see Rom. 8:22–23).

This where God steps in. When we don't know what to pray for, "the Spirit helps us in our weakness" by interceding for us "with groanings too deep for words" (Rom. 8:26). God's Spirit speaks on behalf of our speechless hearts, bringing them into God's presence and interceding for us "according to the will of God" (v. 27). God will hear and answer the Spirit's prayers, and we can be confident that He will continue to work out His good purposes in and through us—the chief of which is transforming us into the image of His Son (see vv. 28–29). And if the Spirit's intercession weren't enough, verse 34 declares that Jesus also intercedes for us!

Romans 8 is a good reminder that prayer isn't an end in itself; it is a means for us to know and commune with our loving heavenly Father. God started the conversation by giving us His Word, and we can respond by praying His Word back to Him, which warms and refines our hearts in the process. We can pour out our hearts before Him in confidence (see Ps. 62:8). There are many proven paths we can take in order to converse with Him—but when our weakness prohibits us from taking them, He doesn't reject us. Instead, He enlists His Son and Spirit to pray on our behalf, ensuring that our weakness (and even our sin) won't have the last word. Thanks be to God!

PRAYER

Father, thank You for starting the conversation by giving us Your Word and sending Your Son for us. You have given us so much to respond to and to take back to You in prayer, it's incredible! Help me to grow in prayer and to pray according to Your Word. Use the prayers of others to teach me to pray, and use me to positively impact the lives of others. And thank You that the Spirit intercedes for me and that my weakness won't hinder the work that You perform in my life for Your glory. In Jesus's name, amen.

QUESTIONS FOR REFLECTION

1. Why is it important for our prayers to be shaped by the text of Scripture? In what ways has this chapter encouraged you to focus on God's Word when you pray?
2. Which, if any, of the suggested paths for prayer have you used before? How have they helped you? Which of the suggested paths for prayer are you most encouraged to try?

3. Do you ever struggle to praise God when you pray instead of quickly going to present your petitions to Him? How has this chapter encouraged you to grow in that area?

4. Read Romans 8:26–30. How does the Holy Spirit's intercession encourage you?

3

i feel too guilty to pray

"There is therefore now no condemnation for those who are in Christ Jesus." —Paul the apostle, Romans 8:1

If you've ever felt too guilty to pray, you're not alone.

While Anita came to faith in Christ at her church's vacation Bible school as a young girl, she has always struggled to pray. Her lackluster prayer life makes her feel guilty. Her friend Brianna prays all the time, and God listens to her; why can't she be like Brianna? But instead of taking her lack of prayer itself to the Lord in prayer, she feels ashamed and shrugs off the thought of praying altogether. "Maybe I'm not a natural pray-er."

Carlos was born again after he visited his coworker's church and heard the gospel. After his conversion, Carlos found prayer to be easy and joyful. But now that he's settled into the Christian life, his sin patterns concern him and make him anxious. "Shouldn't I be over these sins already? Why should God listen to me when I disappoint Him so much?" For Carlos, true prayer seems out of reach until he can get his act together.

Carlos and Anita both demonstrate a common struggle. Guilt

sucks the oxygen out of the room as it relates to their prayer—whether it be guilt over their sin or guilt for not praying as they think God wants them to. Instead of a joy, prayer becomes a burden—another time for them not to measure up. Instead of confidently approaching their loving heavenly Father, they see God as an impossible-to-please taskmaster. Do you ever feel like Carlos or Anita?

"Guilt makes me feel that God doesn't want me to talk to Him," one person whom I surveyed said. Another confessed, "I feel far from God when I sin." "I feel weary and frustrated for sinning in the same way multiple times," said yet another.

Troubled consciences lead many people to feel ashamed and to hide from God, as Adam and Eve did in the garden in Genesis 3. But now that Jesus has come and cleansed us of our sins, we no longer need to hide from God in shame; we can draw near to Him in faith. Forgetting this truth will kill joy in your Christian life.

Puritan Thomas Brooks writes, "It is the devil's logic to argue thus: My sins are great, therefore I will not go to Christ, I dare not rest nor lean on Christ; whereas the soul should reason thus: The greater my sins are, the more I stand in need of mercy, of pardon, and therefore I will go to Christ, who delights in mercy, who pardons sin for his own name's sake."[1]

The cross flips guilt on its head and turns it from a hindrance to prayer into a motivator. In this chapter, we will see what to do with our guilt and then consider how to approach prayer itself.

WHAT DOES GOD REQUIRE OF US?

If you've ever felt guilty because you don't think that you pray the way God wants you to, it's probably a good idea to answer the question "What does God want from us in terms of prayer?"

---

1. Thomas Brooks, *Precious Remedies against Satan's Devices* (1652; repr., Carlisle, PA: Banner of Truth, 2011), 215.

I'll suggest this radically simple answer: *that we pray.*[2] Scripture is filled with many commands for us to pray, but it does not command a specific length of time ("You have to pray at least thirty minutes a day") or a specific routine ("You must pray at such-and-such a time"). Often Scripture's commands for us to pray are accompanied by glorious promises designed to drive us to prayer by reminding us of its amazing results (see Jeremiah 33:3; Matt. 7:7–11; and James 5:16–18 for a few examples). God is not concerned about performance-related statistics; He cares about whether our hearts seek to pray and persevere in approaching Him. Arbitrary measures of perfection should never be our focus. As we will see in the rest of this chapter, knowing and applying the gospel is the best thing we can do to make progress in our struggles with guilt.

GOOD NEWS FOR GUILTY CONSCIENCES

According to the gospel, Jesus removes our guilt. Okay, okay; you know that already. So did Carlos and Anita—but they still let feelings of guilt keep them from praying. Their head knowledge did not match with their heart theology. Has this ever happened to you? It's happened to me—even during entire seasons of my Christian walk.

Instead of trusting Christ's finished work, I've looked to my own performance (or lack thereof). In good times this has led to pride and, in bad, to great discouragement because I could never measure up. When I—and when you—do this, we fail to believe the gospel. We are righteous in Christ alone, and that truth has glorious implications for our prayer.

The writer to the Hebrews shared a truth that has proved to

2. The rest of this book teaches more about what God specifically wants from us when we pray—but in the context of the guilt that we may feel about approaching Him, I'll stick with this simple conclusion!

be a game changer for me, regarding not only my prayer but also my sanctification:

> For we do not have a high priest who is unable to sympathize with our weaknesses, but one who in every respect has been tempted as we are, yet without sin. Let us then with confidence draw near to the throne of grace, that we may receive mercy and find grace to help in time of need. (Heb. 4:15–16)

Jesus sympathizes with our weaknesses, because He experienced temptation Himself. The fact that He was victorious over sin means that He is strong enough to help us overcome our weaknesses. And the logical conclusion of this is that we can draw near to the throne of grace "with confidence."

Oh, how I love that this passage mentions our "time of need"! God knows we have needs and promises to meet them in Christ. If you feel guilty or ashamed of what you have done (or not done) in your life, *congratulations!* You are in a time of need and have a Savior who can perfectly meet your need. You have not been left empty-handed. Your gracious heavenly Father has given you a key to His unlimited storehouse of grace.

FIGHTING AGAINST A GUILTY CONSCIENCE

The fight against a guilty conscience feels like those old cartoons with a character who has a little devil on one shoulder and a little angel on the other. The little devil, pitchfork in hand, shouts lies and accusations in one ear while the angel meekly whispers truth in the other. When the devil's voice is heard ten times louder than the truth, it's hard to ignore!

The great twentieth-century preacher Dr. Martyn Lloyd-Jones prescribes what we need: "We should spend a good deal of time everyday preaching to ourselves and never more than when

[we] get on [our] knees in prayer."[3] When we preach God's Word to ourselves, we use it as the sword of the Spirit to cut down the lies that our hearts and the enemy tell us (see Eph. 6:17). We need constant reminders about the identity we have in Christ and the sufficiency of His work—especially when we're doubting.

Charles Spurgeon provides an example of how to do spiritual battle with gospel truth:

> I know what the devil will say to you. He will say to you, "You are a sinner!" Tell him you know you are, but that . . . you are justified. He will tell you of the greatness of your sin. Tell him of the greatness of Christ's righteousness. He will tell you of all your mishaps and your backslidings, of your offences and your wanderings. Tell him, and tell your own conscience, that you know all that, but that Jesus Christ came to save sinners, and that, although your sin be great, Christ is quite able to put it all away.[4]

Don't focus on your faults; focus on Christ's victory. Trust in His perfect work instead of your faulty work, for "whoever believes in him will not be put to shame" (1 Peter 2:6).

CULTIVATING A GOSPEL MINDSET FOR PRAYER

When guilt hinders our prayers, we are often unconscious of it. Without realizing it, we may drift away from God slowly over time. In order to anchor ourselves in the gospel instead, we need to cultivate habits, through thought and through prayer, that

3. D. Martyn Lloyd-Jones, *The Unsearchable Riches of Christ: An Exposition of Ephesians 3* (Grand Rapids: Baker Books, 1979), 102.

4. C. H. Spurgeon, "Justification by Faith" (sermon, Metropolitan Tabernacle, London, UK, April 28, 1867), available online at https://www.blueletterbible.org/Comm/spurgeon_charles/sermons/3392.cfm.

reflect a humble repentance before God in us as well as a confident trust in Christ's finished work.

Here are several practices that will help us to do just that.

Keep the Cross and the Resurrection Always before Us

Keeping the cross always before us humbles us by reminding us of why Christ died: to pay the penalty for our sins. It also provides us with assurance by reminding us that God doesn't want His redeemed children to be far off and distant; He wants us to enjoy the communion and freedom that come from being His adopted children. Christ's resurrection is the proof that His sacrifice was acceptable to God the Father as well as proof that He is "far above all rule and authority and power and dominion, and above every name that is named, not only in this age but also in the one to come" (Eph. 1:21).

When guilt and shame hurl condemnation at us, let's call to mind the fact that the only all-powerful Being in existence demonstrated His love for us by sending His Son to a cross so that we would be reconciled to Him (see Rom. 5:8–11). Let's remember the conscience-cleansing power of the cross (see Heb. 9:14).

Confess Our Sins

Even though we are blood-bought children of God, our sin offends God and may keep Him from listening to our prayers (see Psalm 66:18).[5]

Maybe you've experienced this feeling of being locked out of the room of prayer. When this happens, examine your life for unconfessed sins and confess them before the Lord—"With this key," John Calvin says, you "open for [yourself] the door to prayer."[6] Cornelius Plantinga writes that "recalling and confessing

5. I will deal more with this point in chapter 4.
6. *Calvin: Institutes of the Christian Religion*, vol. 2, *Books III.XX to IV.XX*, ed. John T. McNeill, trans. Ford Lewis Battles (Philadelphia: The Westminster Press, 1960), 3.20.9.

our sin is like taking out the garbage: once is not enough."[7] If our sin has the ugly potential to shut the ear of God to our prayers, then we're going to need to take out the trash of our spiritual lives by confessing this sin every chance we get. (And, the truth is, neglecting the discipline of confession may be exactly what has led us to our feelings of guilt in the first place!)

When Jesus teaches us in the Lord's Prayer to pray, "Forgive us our debts" (Matt. 6:12), He *invites* us to confess and even shows us that this is His expectation for us as redeemed sinners. Bringing our sin before Christ isn't a shock or disappointment to Him; it's evidence of an obedient and repentant heart. It's exactly what God wants from us.

So let's regularly confess our sins to God with the confidence that He will keep His promise: "If we confess our sins, he is faithful and just to forgive us our sins and to cleanse us from all unrighteousness" (1 John 1:9). Let's confess to God that we are more sinful than we realize and that we need His Spirit to reveal our sin to us so that we can confess and repent.

While confession of our sins to God is of paramount importance, confessing them to other believers has much benefit as well. James writes, "Confess your sins to one another and pray for one another, that you may be healed" (James 5:16). When we confess to one another (along with exercising wisdom about who we confess to), we bring our sin into the light and, as a result, experience the restorative power of confession. After all, God has designed the church to be a gospel community in which we encourage one another to live lives of continual repentance.

Mourn over Our Sins

Unfortunately, our sinful desires may twist promises like 1 John 1:9 when we are quick to confess and move on from our

---

7. Cornelius Plantinga Jr., *Not the Way It's Supposed to Be: A Breviary of Sin* (1995; repr., Grand Rapids: William B. Eerdmans, 1996), x.

sins without seeking true repentance or lasting change. God doesn't want mere drive-thru confession; He wants heart contrition, and He even says that mourning over sin is "blessed" and a path to comfort (Matt. 5:4).

In the second letter we have that he wrote to the Corinthians, Paul speaks of a previous letter he had written to them that had called them out on their sin. His words in that letter had struck the Corinthians like a wrecking ball—and their response to it had provided a stellar example of godly grief over sin:

> For godly grief produces a repentance that leads to salvation without regret, whereas worldly grief produces death. For see what earnestness this godly grief has produced in you, but also what eagerness to clear yourselves, what indignation, what fear, what longing, what zeal, what punishment! At every point you have proved yourselves innocent in the matter. (2 Cor. 7:10–11)

The Corinthians didn't brush off Paul's words or sulk over them; they felt the weight of them. Their only appropriate response was to surrender their emotions to God and commit to changing. The Corinthians proved an important point: even when our sin dishonors God, we can honor Him through our response.

Don't gloss over this point too quickly, lest you fall into what Dietrich Bonhoeffer called "cheap grace."[8] Cheap grace turns the grace of God into a license to sin. Living out true repentance before God involves being deeply affected by the ways we have sinned against Him and grieved His Spirit.

I'm no gardener, but I know that if you cut a weed off at its stalk, it's only a matter of time until the weed will spring up again.

8. See throughout Dietrich Bonhoeffer, "Costly Grace," chap. 1 in *The Cost of Discipleship* (repr., New York: Touchstone, 1995).

Mourning over our sins puts weed killer in the hands of the Spirit and helps us to rid our hearts of our destructive sin-loving tendencies. You may want to take the approach of a pastor I know and pray daily to hate sin and love Christ.

Believe the Gospel and Pray with Confidence

Taking hold of the great promises God has made in the gospel gives us confidence when we pray—confidence that Christ's blood has washed away our sins and confidence that because of Him, our Father hears us.

The following testimony shows how one believer, named Chris, has learned how to overcome his guilty feelings and to boldly enter the throne room of grace.

> Guilt used to impede my prayers constantly. I had no understanding of Hebrews 4:16. I felt I had to "clean myself up" before running to His throne of grace. . . . Rather than impede, my guilt now compels me to run to Christ. When my feelings do not match up with my identity in Christ, He is the only place for me to go to find the grace to deal with it. Since God is no longer holding my sins against me (see 2 Cor. 5:19), it is only the enemy or my flesh that tries to convince me that my failures should impede my running to Christ. The biblical answer is the opposite. . . . The more I trust in Christ's righteousness rather than my own, the less my guilt impedes my prayer and the more it pushes me into it every single time.

FREE, IN CHRIST, TO PRAY

Remember Carlos and Anita from the beginning of this chapter? By God's grace, they have both been learning how to fight guilt with the gospel. And they have grown.

Anita no longer lets her failures in prayer dictate her relationship with God; instead, she has found that meditating on the gracious heart of her Father draws her into deeper and more joyful communion with Him. She remembers that God hears her not because she's eloquent in prayer but because she has God's perfect Son as her Advocate (see 1 John 2:1–2).

When the devil hurls accusations at Carlos about his sin, he fights back by remembering the gospel. "I knew intellectually the gospel was good news," Carlos confessed. "But I didn't understand how it could help me fight sin. Now, instead of running from God because of guilt, I bring my guilt before Him. Not only do I know I am cleansed, but I am invigorated to press on in the gospel because of what Jesus has done for me."

PRAYER

Dear heavenly Father, thank You for Jesus! Thank You for Your love for sinners. I am in awe that You could care for a rebellious soul like me. Help me to live all of life with the cross in mind. Help me to battle feelings of guilt with gospel truths, and give me great joy as I grow each day in the realization of the unsearchable riches of Christ that are mine (see Eph. 3:8)! In Jesus's name, amen.

QUESTIONS FOR REFLECTION

1. Have feelings of guilt impeded your prayer life before? If so, how?
2. How does thinking of God as your heavenly Father, instead of as a harsh taskmaster, change your attitude toward prayer?
3. When guilt impedes our prayer lives, it's often because we trust our feelings more than the Word of God. How

can you grow in the area of letting the Word of God shape your feelings of guilt?

4. Of the four steps this chapter covered for cultivating a gospel mindset in prayer, which do you think you need to work the hardest on implementing?

4

i'm not sure God hears me

"How long, O LORD? Will you forget me forever?
How long will you hide your face from me?"
—David, Psalm 13:1

Have you ever had a good friend disappear? Not a back-of-the-milk-carton kind of disappear, but a call-them-repeatedly-and-not-get-a-response kind of disappear? When this first happens, you're surprised—*Weren't we good friends who had great times together?* But as time goes on and you keep reaching out, you realize that you may never get a response. *They're just too busy for me or not interested in a relationship anymore.*

Have you ever felt this way about God? You pray, you attend church, you read your Bible, and you encourage friends in the faith. But God seems eerily silent. You're not sure that your prayers have reached God. And if they have reached Him, you're not sure that they're important to Him—as if each prayer were another piece of mail piling up on His already cluttered desk.

"I have never felt like he wasn't listening," wrote one survey responder, "but I have felt like it didn't matter—that he didn't care."

Maybe you understand that He cares but struggle because you haven't received the answer you were looking for. This is especially painful when you cry out repeatedly for deliverance from a trial, healing for a loved one, or provision in a time of need. When this happens, doubt and discouragement can quickly creep in, causing you to conclude, "I don't think God is listening to me, so I won't pray." But that creates a vicious cycle, because not praying is the only guarantee that He won't hear you! Some people even walk away from faith in Jesus when they don't hear back from God according to their expectations. But faith is exactly what you and I need to get through these frustrating times of silence.

If you've ever felt as if God isn't listening, you're not alone. In fact, you're just like every other Christian! Job knew this experience well. So did David, a man after God's own heart, who prayed in the Psalms, "How long, O LORD?" (Ps. 13:1)! Habakkuk the prophet also cried, "O LORD, how long shall I cry for help, and you will not hear? Or cry to you 'Violence!' and you will not save?" (Hab. 1:2). Don't discount these frustrated cries—the dual authorship of the Scriptures means that it wasn't only Job or David or Habakkuk penning these prayers but also the Holy Spirit Himself. God knows your frustration and gives you words to pray, and examples to follow, when you feel alone in the dark.

Why do we sometimes experience silence from God? Is God cruel? Does He just like to mess with us? Or are there other reasons and greater purposes in God's mind that we don't know about?

WHY HE MAY NOT LISTEN

Thankfully, there are *some* easy answers when you feel as if God isn't receiving your prayers.[1] Let's look at them.

1. This isn't the same as when God doesn't *answer* our prayers—there are other reasons why He might choose to do that. When He doesn't *listen* to us, it is likely because our sin has caused offense to Him and hindered our prayers.

You Aren't a Christian

In chapter 1, we saw how Jesus gives us the confidence to pray and makes God accessible to sinners. One of the scariest truths found in the Bible is that many people *think* they have saving faith in Jesus Christ but actually don't. Jesus warned about fake believers in Matthew 7:21: "Not everyone who says to me, 'Lord, Lord,' will enter the kingdom of heaven." People like this may have grown up in church, know all the right answers to theological questions, be the first to arrive at church on Sunday, and act like Christians outwardly. But they remain unbelievers, and thus God has no obligation to listen to their prayers.

If you have no desire to know God through prayer, examine yourself to see whether you are in the faith (see 2 Cor. 13:5). The desire to pray is hardwired into the soul of the believer. Does it pain you to know you have sinned against a holy God? Do you put your trust in Jesus for the forgiveness of your sins? If you question the veracity of your faith, trust in Jesus—He turns no one away who comes to Him in faith and repentance.

You Lack Faith

Prayer without faith isn't prayer; it's talking to ourselves. Don't forget that "without faith it is *impossible* to please" God (Heb. 11:6). *Impossible* doesn't come with qualifiers. Faithless prayer displeases God. James 1:7–8 says that the doubter "must not suppose that he will receive anything from the Lord; he is a double-minded man, unstable in all his ways."

When we go on autopilot during prayer and merely recite words while thinking about something else, we lack faith. When we ask God for something legitimate but are convinced that He won't answer, we lack faith. The same is true when we pray in order to be seen by others—we put our focus on the reactions of people instead of on God.

Instead of praying this way, simply look to your heavenly

61

Father, trust the promises of His Word, which help to stir your faith (see Rom. 10:17), and speak to Him.

You've Turned Your Back on God and His Word by Embracing Sin

Just as a child's deliberate disobedience grieves his or her father, our sin grieves God (see Eph. 4:30). The psalmist wrote, "If I had cherished iniquity in my heart, the Lord would not have listened" (Ps. 66:18). Our sin shapes the attitudes we have about God and our motives for praying.[2] Living in sin is the opposite of loving God, for "the fear of the LORD is hatred of evil" (Prov. 8:13). Proverbs 28:9 says this truth in a different way: "If one turns away his ear from hearing [God's] law, even his prayer is an abomination."

If you find yourself treasuring sin and avoiding God's Word, repent! And then ask Him to create in you a clean heart and a right spirit (see Ps. 51:10). Confess your sins to God, and to a trusted friend, and start praying again.

You've Treated Others Wrongly

If breaking the Greatest Commandment, by not loving God (see Matt. 22:36–38), can hinder your prayers (as the last point taught), it shouldn't be a surprise that breaking the second Great Commandment, by not loving others (Matt. 22:39), can as well. This is essentially cherishing sin in your heart (see Ps. 66:18) regarding your duties toward other people.

The Bible explicitly identifies the marriage relationship as one place where this may happen. First Peter 3:7 says, "Husbands, live with your wives in an understanding way, showing honor to the woman as the weaker vessel, since they are heirs with you of the grace of life, *so that your prayers may not be hindered.*" At first

---

2. We will say more about motives in the next chapter.

this seems kind of random. Why would God hinder the prayers of knucklehead husbands? The reason is that He wants to lead them to repentance so that they will better care for their wives and honor Him more in their marriages. (While this is not explicitly stated in Scripture, I think that if a wife does not fulfill her role in marriage, her prayers have the potential to be hindered as well, because she is likely treasuring sin.)

The Bible is also explicit in saying that our prayer also may be hindered when we do not offer forgiveness and reconciliation (see Matthew 5:23–24; Mark 11:25; see also 1 Tim. 2:8) or when we neglect our duty to the poor (see Prov. 21:13).

You Are Prideful

The parable of the Pharisee and the tax collector found in Luke 18:9–14 contrasts two postures that we can take toward prayer. The Pharisee strutted around like a spiritual giant, flexing his spiritual muscles and praying, "God, I thank you that I am not like other men, extortioners, unjust, adulterers, or even like this tax collector. I fast twice a week; I give tithes of all that I get" (vv. 11–12). He approached God on the basis of his works, not God's mercy. But God doesn't want us to pat ourselves on the back for how good we are; He wants humble hearts from us that understand our continual need for grace. That's what the tax collector's prayer reflected: "God, be merciful to me, a sinner!" (v. 13).

Jesus's conclusion to this parable sent shock waves to those who were listening: God accepted the socially unacceptable tax collector's prayer while rejecting the admired Pharisee's self-righteous prayer. "For everyone who exalts himself will be humbled, but the one who humbles himself will be exalted" (v. 14).

You Are Experiencing God's Discipline

Knowing God as our Father means that we receive the Father's loving discipline. Receiving God's loving discipline might mean not hearing from Him as we'd expect. He may want to convict us of sin, test us to see what is in our hearts, or cause us to seek Him more fervently; but His firm and gracious hand always has our growth and our good in mind—even when He doesn't answer us as we'd like him to. Realizing this allows you to say, along with H. B. Charles Jr., "God has done great things in my life through an unanswered prayer."[3]

NO SUCH THING AS UNANSWERED PRAYER

There is a crucial difference between God rejecting our prayers, for the aforementioned reasons, and God not answering our prayers. I'm convinced there is no such thing as an unanswered prayer for a Christian.

God is the perfect Father, and we are His beloved children. What earthly father would reject the pleading of his child? Not a good one. And yet what earthly father always immediately answers his child's request in exactly the way that the child wants? One who is either shortsighted, lazy, or both. But our heavenly Father is good and is not shortsighted or lazy. He always has greater purposes than simply being a genie who will grant our wishes. God always answers our prayers but often doesn't do so in the timing we want or the ways we prefer. His answers may come as a "Yes," or a "No," or a "Wait."

The waiting is the hardest part. I can usually deal with a no. But waiting for answers to life's deepest prayers hurts. Will my loved one ever follow Christ? Will healing ever come? Will I ever get the new job that I need so badly?

Even if all we hear is crickets, having confidence in the love and sovereignty of God will provide us with fertile ground for persevering prayers.

3. H. B. Charles Jr., "How You Handle Answered Prayers" (sermon, Shiloh Metropolitan Baptist Church, Jacksonville, FL, January 20, 2016).

LEARNING TO TRUST OUR GRACIOUS GOD AND HIS ETERNAL PURPOSES

For as the heavens are higher than the earth,
  so are my ways higher than your ways
  and my thoughts than your thoughts. (Isa. 55:9)

These words provide us much comfort when we don't understand what God is up to. My thoughts and ways are often self-centered and shortsighted. I crave immediate relief and a sense of God's presence. But even when it seems God is giving me the silent treatment, He is at work.

My friend Jeff hit rock bottom when he lost his job. He had cried out for God to provide that job for over two years—why would God take it away so quickly? Didn't He know that Jeff needed to provide for his wife and four children? Didn't He know about the escalating medical bills from his entire family's battle with Lyme disease, his wife's degenerative ankle, and his son's behavioral issues?

"As I poured myself into finding a new job, I prayed—no, pleaded—for God to intervene." Jeff shared.

But the Lord delayed. I had to wait, month after month, with seemingly no end in sight. Many several-month-long interview processes which pointed to promising outcomes all ended with doors being shut in unexpected ways.

Waiting was hard. God's "no"s were confusing when we were in such genuine need. But, looking back, I can now see how it drove me to a deeper dependence on Christ for each step, along with greater confidence in his provision for our family. In time, he provided a new job—and by the time he did, I was a profoundly different person.[4]

4. Jeff Walton shared this in the book he cowrote with his wife, Sarah, *Together Through the Storms: Biblical Encouragements for Your Marriage When Life Hurts* (Char-

Believers who are in circumstances like Jeff's face the temptation to turn inward in self-pity, grow bitter, and even echo the sentiment of Job's wife: "Curse God and die!" (Job 2:9 NASB). But abiding in Christ while we wait for an answer activates His gracious hand to prune unfruitful branches from our lives and mold us into the image of His Son.

> I still long for relief and healing for my son and my family, and I did really need a job to provide for them, but the waiting increased my longing for more of Christ and his glory through our lives, even at the cost of earthly comfort. That would never have happened if Jesus had healed my son as a toddler or answered when I first prayed for a job. He has loved me enough to delay. And he has loved me enough to allow the death of so much in me (my strength, comfort, desire for success, and self-confidence) in order to bring me greater life in him and bring glory to himself.[5]

Suffering through God's silence is often the best way for us to learn what true prayer is—dependence on our Savior who holds all things together (see Col. 1:17). God doesn't want us to pray in order to manipulate Him into accomplishing our will; He wants to mold us into the image of His Son and hear us cry from the heart, "Your will be done!"

"Developing a relationship with us is God's goal," explains W. Bingham Hunter, "and answers to prayer are a means he uses to foster self-disclosure, growth and understanding of both him and ourselves. Since we are given to longer petitions than thanksgivings, it may be that for God to answer our prayers immediately might help depersonalize our thinking about him and be counterproductive to growth in our relationship with him."[6]

---

lotte: The Good Book Company, 2020), 112.

5. Walton and Walton, 114.

6. W. Bingham Hunter, *The God Who Hears* (Downers Grove, IL: IVP Books, 1986), 79.

HIS GRACE IS SUFFICIENT FOR YOU NO MATTER WHAT

In 2 Corinthians 12, the apostle Paul describes an experience during which God gave him a glimpse into "the third heaven," which is also described as "paradise" (vv. 2–3). But Paul reports only that "he heard things that cannot be told, which man may not utter" (v. 4)—and after this incredible experience, he didn't write any books or go on a speaking tour. Instead, he returned home to an unwelcome surprise.

God allowed a thorn in Paul's flesh—a "messenger of Satan" to harass him (v. 7). While we don't know exactly what this thorn was—a thorn of physical affliction, of spiritual weakness, of an unnecessary committee at church, or of another painful addition to his life—we do know God's purpose behind giving it to Paul: to keep him from becoming conceited (see v. 7). (If I took a trip to heaven, I'd walk with a strut in my step, myself!) Like any good Christian, Paul cried out three times for God to remove the thorn. God didn't. Instead, He replied, "My grace is sufficient for you, for my power is made perfect in weakness" (v. 9).

God was allowing Paul to experience affliction instead of a swelling pride. I imagine that God's response hit Paul like a ton of bricks. I would have said to Him, "God, don't You care about my suffering?" But God's response changed Paul in a way that allowed the power of Christ to rest upon him (see vv. 9–10). After contemplating the depths of the infinite sufficiency of the grace of God, Paul could boast in his weakness with the knowledge that his pain would bring God glory.

There is never a moment in your entire life when God's grace is not sufficient for you. There is no physical trial, no spiritual battle, no emotional pain during which God will abandon you. He is working in your life, as he did in Paul's, to conform you to the image of His Son.

Paul knew God's ultimate purpose for saying no to his prayers. But you and I may never understand, on earth, what God's purpose is for our trials. And that's okay. We can live and pray with the confidence that God will not waste our efforts in prayer or whatever trial we are experiencing. We can trust that He will work all things for the good of those who love Him (see Rom. 8:28)—even if we have to wait until eternity to taste this "good" that comes from our circumstances.[7]

KEEP AN ETERNAL PERSPECTIVE

The movie *A Hidden Life* tells the true story of Franz Jägerstätter, an Austrian farmer who refused to serve in Hitler's army during World War II because of his faith in Christ. Throughout the movie you see him in prayer—sometimes as he is praying words from the Lord's Prayer while in custody. The movie showcases the tremendous suffering and pain of Franz and his family. Many characters recommend that he accept a noncombat position, like that of a medic, to save himself from his eventual execution—but he stands firm till the end and gives his life because of it.

One heart-wrenching scene involves a fellow prisoner who taunts the suffering Jägerstätter with these words: "How far we are from having our daily bread! How far from being delivered from evil!"—as if to say that suffering at the hands of the Third Reich nullifies the idea that God answers prayers.[8] *A Hidden Life's* portrayal of Jägerstätter's story even led one movie critic to say a key point of the film is that "God does not answer prayers."[9] What

7. I like what Paul Miller says: "How boring life would be if prayer worked like magic. There'd be no relationship with God, no victory over little pockets of evil." Paul E. Miller, *A Praying Life: Connecting with God in a Distracting World*, rev. ed. (Colorado Springs: NavPress, 2017), 203.

8. Scene 20 of *A Hidden Life*, directed by Terrence Malick (2019; Beverly Hills, CA: Twentieth Century Fox Home Entertainment, 2020), DVD.

9. Erik Henriksen, "The First Half of Terrence Malick's *A Hidden Life* Is Great,"

this critic, as well as many believers, fail to recognize is that God works on the landscape of eternity.

We see this again with the apostle Paul, who faced a similar situation to Franz and, like Franz, ultimately gave his life for Christ. At the end of his last letter, Paul was able to boldly proclaim, "The Lord will rescue me from every evil deed and bring me safely into his heavenly kingdom" (2 Tim. 4:18). And yet, soon after he wrote those words, the Roman empire executed Paul. That doesn't seem like a rescue!

But an eternal perspective remembers that *nothing*—not the Third Reich, not the Roman Empire, nor any future enemy—can separate us from the love of God in Jesus Christ (see Rom. 8:38–39). Ultimately God used the deaths of Franz Jägerstätter and of the apostle Paul as the means of their rescue—as the vehicle to transport them into eternal life with their Savior. Death is a conquered enemy (see 1 Cor. 15:54–58). Death is the end of our road of suffering and the beginning of pleasures that we will experience forevermore in God's presence (see Ps. 16:11).

TOWARD A HUMBLE AND JOYFUL SUBMISSION

While in the garden the night before His crucifixion, the Lord Jesus Christ prayed three times for God to deliver Him from the suffering of the cross: "My Father, if it be possible, let this cup pass from me; nevertheless, not as I will, but as you will" (Matt. 26:39). Yet God the Father answered no to the prayer of God the Son. And praise God that He did! The Son's holy submission to the will of the Father made our redemption possible. He could endure the cross "for the joy that was set before him" (Heb. 12:2)—Jesus had a long-term view of what God was

---

Blogtown, Portland Mercury, December 20, 2019, https://www.portlandmercury.com/blogtown/2019/12/20/27668144/the-first-half-of-terrence-malicks-a-hidden-life-is-great.

accomplishing through His intense suffering. When we realize how God works and stand upon the unshakable promises of the gospel, we can more easily and joyfully submit ourselves to the will of our loving heavenly Father.

I love how W. Bingham Hunter put it:

> No matter how large a spiritual giant you may become, there will be days when God's answer to your prayers will be no. Despite your seeking, searching, and the outpouring of your soul, your heavenly Father has decided against your petition. When this happens your *attitude* becomes the vital factor. Are you willing to give your hurt, disappointment, perhaps even grief, to Christ who died for you . . . and then begin to pray again? Prayer problems are usually not intellectual, but volitional. In praying effectively the submission of your will is directly linked with finding God's will. Prayer which God answers is always offered with an attitude of submission.[10]

What incredible hope we have, even in frustrating times! We have an all-wise God who provides sufficient grace to meet all our needs. He may *seem* not to hear us at times, but we can keep calling out to Him in confidence and hope, with the knowledge that we will marvel at His wisdom, justice, and tender care for all eternity. Praise be to God!

PRAYER

Dear heavenly Father, thank You for hearing my prayers even though I don't always feel like You do and for answering my prayers even if I don't always like Your answers. Please expose the sin in my life that keeps me from You. Deepen my trust in your

---

10. Hunter, *The God Who Hears*, 65.

sufficient grace and glorious sovereignty. I praise You that even though I wait and suffer in this life, I can always trust in how You are working all things for my good (see Rom. 8:28). Help me to be steadfast in prayer for Your glory. In Jesus's name, amen.

QUESTIONS FOR REFLECTION

1. Have you ever gone through a season when it seems like God is distant and not hearing your prayer? If so, why did it seem this way, and how might this chapter shed light on that struggle?
2. How has waiting on God for answers challenged you? Made you more like Christ?
3. How might the truth that God's grace is sufficient for you impact the worst fears that you have in this life?
4. What if God answered every one of your prayers—but not in this lifetime? How would that change your prayers?

5

i have mixed motives

"All the ways of a man are pure in his own eyes,
but the Lord weighs the spirit." —Solomon, Proverbs 16:2

"Kevin hit me back!" My sister Kelly ran to tell my mom these words after an "altercation" we had as preschool-aged kids. Tattling about my sin, unbeknownst to my sister, revealed her own sin—that she had started our spat in the first place! And now her humorous words live on in Halloran family lore.

Our prayers can reveal sin within us in a similar way. James, the brother of Jesus, mentioned in his epistle not one but two struggles we have that are related to prayer. The first struggle is the greatest of all: prayerlessness. "You do not have, because you do not ask" (James 4:2). And the next verse shares another major struggle regarding prayer: praying with impure motives. "You ask and do not receive, because you ask wrongly, to spend it on your passions" (v. 3). James wrote these words to address a conflict in the church. Quarrels, fights, and wars abounded because of this conflict (see v. 1)[1]—which was the natural result of the selfish

---

1. Since James wrote to "the twelve tribes in the Dispersion" (v. 1), it was likely a pattern of conflict across many churches rather than a specific one.

ambition and jealously that waged war within his readers (see James 3:14–16). And sinful passions like the ones James was writing about not only cause conflict with our fellow man but also breed conflict with God.

When we're looking at the sinful motives behind our prayers, we need to look at their root causes. James mentions several sins that lie behind wrong motives: bitter jealousy, selfish ambition, covetousness, and disorder. We could express any of these sins by asking for something with wrong motives or for selfish reasons—such as for a Ferrari or a winning lottery ticket. We can even ask for something that is seemingly *good* with the wrong motives, such as relational blessings or a bigger ministry. Do I want relational blessings simply in order to make my life easier? Is my desire for a bigger ministry for God's renown or for my own? It's often harder to detect when we are asking for good things with wrong motives—as one missionary named Derrick confessed to me, "I can make things look like godly needs, but in my heart of hearts, I know there's ill motivation somewhere down there." And Eugene Peterson writes that "everything that is disreputable in us—lust, avarice, pride, pettiness—disguises itself in prayer."[2]

How can we uncover the sinful motives that lurk behind our prayers so we don't say the equivalent of "Kevin hit me back!" to God? How can we honor Him when we aren't sure of our motives? These are the questions we will answer in this chapter.

THREE QUESTIONS FOR DIAGNOSING OUR MOTIVES

Discerning our motives isn't always cut-and-dried. As justified sinners, we should always be suspicious of our sinful hearts. "The

2. Eugene H. Peterson, *Answering God: The Psalms as Tools for Prayer* (1989; repr., San Francisco: Harper San Francisco, 1991), 5.

temptation to misuse prayer is native to us and comes . . . automatically to every believer," writes Ole Hallesby.[3]

Our goal behind evaluating our motives should also be to have a pure heart before God—not necessarily to have prayers answered according to our liking.

The following diagnostic questions overlap a bit, because it's easier to expose dirty motives by shining light on them from several angles. If you can't answer the following questions in the affirmative, then your prayers are out of bounds and it's time to check your heart.

1. Am I Praying for God's Glory?

God calls us to do all things for His glory (see 1 Cor. 10:31)—including prayer. This is why Jesus teaches us that "whatever you ask in my name, this I will do, *that the Father may be glorified in the Son*" (John 14:13). When we pray for our own glory, we clash with God's purposes and exalt ourselves over Him. And our sinful motives often disguise themselves so well that we think we're seeking God's glory when we aren't.

W. Bingham Hunter describes one subtle way of secretly seeking your own glory as "praying with *faith in your faith*."[4] This type of prayer twists the good promise of answered prayer into a formula. *If I pray with enough faith, I will get what I want!* And this not only doesn't glorify God but also doesn't often work. Hunter explains how praying this way leads to frustration:

> When the answer is not forthcoming, we are left only with questions: Did I have enough faith? Did my friends who prayed with me have enough faith? Should I have fasted or perhaps claimed a different promise? Attention is centered on prayer

3. O. Hallesby, *Prayer*, trans. Clarence J. Carlsen, updated ed. (Minneapolis: Augsburg Fortress, 1994), 122.
4. W. Bingham Hunter, *The God Who Hears* (Downers Grove, IL: IVP Books, 1986), 161.

methods and techniques for generating faith. Thoughts center on us. Then they begin to shift with measurable envy toward those who apparently had enough faith: Why him or her and not me? The progression may end in speculations about the reality of God's love, justice and goodness. The results? We feel alienated from ourselves: we have too little faith. We feel alienated from others: they had enough faith. And we feel alienated from God who set up such a system in the first place. Essentially we are telling God how to glorify himself in our lives . . . and he wouldn't do it.[5]

Praying for God's glory means letting His sovereign wisdom decide what to do with your prayers and your life. It means keeping our focus on Him and on His glory over our own. "Prayer is not a convenient device for imposing our will upon God, or for bending his will to ours, but the prescribed way of subordinating our will to his."[6] When we can't pray and mean "Your will be done," we are essentially telling God "My will be done."

A few questions will help you to evaluate whether you are praying for God's glory:

- Would the desired answer to your prayer cause God's name to be praised?
- Would your desired answer to this prayer bring you closer to God or push you away from Him?
- How would your desired answer to this prayer impact others? Would it help you to love them more?
- Would Jesus pray this prayer in the same situation?[7]

---

5. Hunter, 161–62.

6. John R. W. Stott, *The Letters of John: An Introduction and Commentary*, rev. ed., Tyndale New Testament Commentaries (Grand Rapids: William B. Eerdmans, 1988), 188.

7. This last question is a paraphrase of Hunter in *The God Who Hears*, 198.

2. Am I Praying in Line with Scripture?

This question provides a helpful litmus test for our motives. If we ever pray for something that's forbidden in Scripture (and thus outside of God's will), we cannot expect to receive the answer we're hoping for—and we likely have an idol in our lives to repent of. R.C. Sproul exposes one particularly heinous way of doing this:

> Professing Christians often ask God to bless or sanction their sin. They are even capable of telling their friends they have prayed about a certain matter and God has given them peace despite what they prayed for was contrary to His will. Such prayers are thinly veiled acts of blasphemy, and we add insult to God when we dare to announce that His Spirit has sanctioned our sin by giving us peace in our souls. Such a peace is a carnal peace and has nothing to do with the peace that passes understanding, the peace that the Spirit is pleased to grant to those who love God and love His law.[8]

Don't miss Sproul's last point: peace isn't from God if it's a "peace" we're feeling when our actions are flying in the face of scriptural truth. We should weigh every prayer and every motive against God's Word.[9] When we are clearly at odds with the Word, we need to repent. When we aren't sure, we need to ask God to reveal sin in us and to consider what negative desires and powerful emotions may be warping our prayers.

3. Am I Pursuing Humility and Holiness?

After James explains the danger of praying with impure motives, he shares how we can repent of them. He quotes from

---

8. R.C. Sproul, *The Invisible Hand: Do All Things Really Work for Good?* (1996; repr., Phillipsburg, NJ: P&R, 2003), 209, quoted in Paul Tautges, *Brass Heavens: Reasons for Unanswered Prayer* (Adelphi, MD: Cruciform Press, 2013), 27.

9. It's also worth mentioning here the utility of regularly praying Scripture, which

Proverbs, which says that "God opposes the proud but gives grace to the humble" (James 4:6; cf. Prov. 3:34), and then he presents this litany of commands:

> Submit yourselves therefore to God.
>
> Resist the devil, and he will flee from you.
>
> Draw near to God, and he will draw near to you.
>
> Cleanse your hands, you sinners, and purify your hearts, you double-minded.
>
> Be wretched and mourn and weep.
>
> Let your laughter be turned to mourning and your joy to gloom. (James 4:7–9)

And then he closes with what ties everything he's been saying all together: "Humble yourselves before the Lord, and he will exalt you" (v. 10). Essentially, James sandwiches commands to repent between two calls to humility.

Being humble before God is a key part of testing our motives, because it (1) recognizes that our motives may be out of whack and (2) acknowledges that God both knows our sinful motives and is able to reveal them to us. If we want to properly discern our motives, we need to pursue humility and holiness, because a life of sin and pride will cloud our spiritual vision and make it difficult for us to discern our true motives.

James commands holiness and reconciliation with God. The "double-minded" person mentioned in James 1:8 is someone who claims to love God but *actually* loves sin. James says in verses 7

---

helps us to keep our hearts and motives tied to the truth of the Word. Doing so is a prayer-filtering mechanism that makes discerning our motives easier and more automatic.

and 8 that a double-minded person is unstable in his ways and
"must not suppose that he will receive anything from the Lord."
Does sin have a grip on your heart? Those who love Jesus keep
His commandments (see John 14:15). In humility, repent of any
double-mindedness in your life and pursue God as your greatest
love. A healthy life of prayer must never be divorced from a faithful life of Christian obedience.[10]

THE SAFEGUARD OF PRUDENCE

Prudence is "caution or circumspection as to danger or risk."[11] If
we apply that definition to the context of discerning the motives
behind our prayers, prudence means taking great care in approaching God when we suspect that our motives may be out of sync
with His Spirit. We especially need to take care regarding how we
pray and how we think in intense, emotionally charged situations.

Pastor and professor Bryan Chapell describes an experience
he and his wife had while driving through a snowstorm on a dan-
gerous road.[12] The heavy snow was nearly blinding them from
seeing in front of them, but they were fortunate enough to see fenceposts lining both sides of the road. Although they couldn't see
far into the distance, keeping their eye on those fenceposts told
them they were headed in the right direction—and were still on
the road! Just as the fenceposts kept Dr. Chapell and his wife safe
as they moved forward in the snowstorm, our focus on holiness
and prudence will keep us from veering off the road into a ditch
of bad motives when we pray.

10. It's always worth mentioning that God's laws are for our joy and good and by
nature are not burdensome. See John 15:7–11; 1 John 5:3.

11. *Merriam-Webster's Collegiate Dictionary*, 11th ed. (2003), s.v. "prudence."

12. Dr. Bryan Chapell tells this story in *Praying Backwards: Transform Your Prayer
Life by Beginning in Jesus' Name* (Grand Rapids: Baker Books, 2005), 141–42, and I use
it for the same purpose of calling righteousness (I use the word *holiness*) and prudence
as the two fence posts that keep us praying on the road of God's will.

David provides a great example of careful prudence in the face of unknown motives in Psalm 139. In this psalm, he praises God for His intimate knowledge of every detail of David's existence—from conception onward. In the fifth stanza, he calls upon God to destroy His enemies and uses some heated words: "Oh that you would slay the wicked, O God!" (v. 19) and "I hate [Your enemies] with a complete hatred" (v. 22). But before David finishes his prayer, he asks God to test his heart and make sure he hasn't stepped out of bounds with what he has prayed.

> Search me, O God, and know my heart!
>> Try me and know my thoughts!
> And see if there be any grievous way in me,
>> and lead me in the way everlasting! (Ps. 139:23–24)

David knew that God knew him. He knew David's every thought, even when he railed against evildoers, and David invited God's testing ("try me and know my thoughts") and guidance ("lead me in the way everlasting"). He exercised prudence and wanted God's continual, cleansing and purifying power to help him ward off the missteps he had the potential to make in his prayers and his life.

When you can't discern the motives of your heart, pray Psalm 139:23–24. Pray Psalm 19:14, as well, which says, "Let the words of my mouth and the meditation of my heart be acceptable in your sight, O Lord, my rock and my redeemer." Remember the glorious promise from James 1:5 that wisdom from God is always available in abundance if you just ask for it. Share with your spouse or a trusted friend or pastor about your mixed motives so that they can shed extra light on the situation. When I prudently seek God's insight into my motives, it rarely takes long for Him to reveal sin and to show me how to think.

Sometimes asking ourselves those diagnostic questions above

will filter out our bad motives and make them obvious. Other times, our motives remain more ambiguous—"I *think* I'm praying rightly, but I don't know for sure." In such times, we have to humbly walk the road of holiness and prudence and trust that God will lead us.

CONTINUING TO PRAY WHEN YOU'RE UNSURE OF YOUR MOTIVES

When my daughter was a toddler, she loved walking to the park down the street. I loved watching her run down the sidewalk and squeal in joy as she anticipated reaching our destination. Her goofy smile, staccato steps, and arms spread wide as if she were giving the whole world a hug always warmed my heart. Yet even though the park is close, the path presents a few dangers for a toddler. There's a street to cross, and it's a main artery for our neighborhood that has more traffic than our own street does. The crosswalk lies at a point where cars from the left come around a blind curve while cars from the right come over a hill, so drivers who are approaching from either direction have little time to react to excited toddlers crossing the road. Once you successfully cross the street, the next potential danger is a pond, whose wildlife is especially enticing to a little girl.

I would have been crazy to let my two-year-old daughter walk to the park on her own—there were too many dangers and she was too inexperienced. But when her mom and I walked with her, she was safe, because we grabbed her before she darted into the street or got too close to the pond to say hi to the "patos" (which means "ducks" in Spanish). Even if she took several strides toward danger, we always grabbed her in time and brought her back to the path to ensure her safe arrival at our destination. God does the same for us when our motives stray as we're praying.

Consider my wife's friend Liza. She struggled with her motives behind the desire she felt to accept a potential opportunity to serve as a trustee in her local government. Did she want the role in order to serve God and others, or for the sake of personal prestige? And she had plenty of excuses for saying no: She didn't have any experience in government and hated the spotlight. She didn't want to spend more time away from her family and didn't want to feel like eyes were always on her. To say no might have also reflected good motives, if she did it out of fear that the opportunity would take her away from her family too much—or it might have reflected *bad* motives, if it was a way of fleeing from God's calling the way Jonah did. Aware that her motives had the potential to be polluted, she placed the situation at the Lord's feet in prayer.

As she sought the Lord's will over the following days, He spoke to her through a specific verse in His Word—Esther 4:14, in which Mordecai tells Esther, "Who knows whether you have not come to the kingdom for such a time as this?" Liza told us, "I had just run into that verse, as I read the Bible in the middle of my decision-making, when *it began to haunt me wherever I went.* In a store, there it was in a frame. In a sermon, it was the center of the message. I saw it on social media and heard it on the radio. A friend sent me a text with that verse without knowing my situation. It became clear—and I soon realized I would be a Jonah if I ran from this opportunity to serve."

God won't always lead us in such obvious ways as He led Liza (although it is nice when He does!). Sometimes He simply wants us to take a step of faith and trust Him when our motives are unclear. Liza's story reminds us that the Lord is our Good Shepherd who leads us "in paths of righteousness for his name's sake" (Ps. 23:3). If we stay on the path of God's will by living righteously for Him, and take care how we engage Him in prayer, He will lead us in what is right. He will do so for our sakes, because He loves us as His children, and He will do so for His name's sake, because guiding a wandering child away from danger brings glory to His name.

THE WORST POSSIBLE TAKEAWAY
FROM THIS CHAPTER

Hopefully this chapter has taught you how to think—and pray—through potentially flawed motives. But there is one reaction you could have to this chapter that would make me wish I had never written it: if you finish it with such a fear of praying with bad motives that you don't pray at all.

If we let fear guide our lives instead of trusting in God, then we miss being led by Him. My daughter would have never experienced the joys of the park if we'd hunkered down at home to avoid danger. And our friend Liza would have missed out on a great chance for her to grow in Christ, and be a light for Him in a dark world, if fear had paralyzed her.

Even when we don't know what our motives are, if we are following the Good Shepherd, living by the light of His Word (see Ps. 119:105), and humbly examining ourselves as we pray, He will lead us on a path that is well lit. God is at work in our lives when we don't know how to pray—and even when we pray wrongly. His Son and Spirit intercede for us according to His will (see Rom. 8:26, 34), and they will filter—and even *correct*—tainted prayers.

Don't let the fear of bad motives keep you from prayer. Pray on in humble confidence.

PRAYER

Father, my sinful heart often tricks me into praying with bad motives. Rid me of these bad motives and teach me what it means to pray—and to live—for Your glory and with the right motives. Thank You that Your Word is like a compass that shows us the direction our hearts need to go, and thank You for protecting me from getting far off track when I pray. Be my delight and greatest joy. In Jesus's name, amen.

QUESTIONS FOR REFLECTION

1. In what ways have you been tempted to pray selfish prayers?
2. What are some of the sins behind the sin of praying with bad motives?
3. How can praying Scripture be a remedy for praying with false motives?
4. Why shouldn't the fear of praying with bad motives keep us from praying?

6

i can't focus

*"The harder we find concentration to be,
the more strenuously we ought to labor after it."*
—*John Calvin*, Institutes of the Christian Religion

Out of all the struggles I have in prayer, a lack of focus may be the greatest.

I do most of my prayer in the morning, with my Bible on my lap, a highlighter in one hand, and coffee in the other. One morning I began my prayer time—and, before I knew it, I had gone to the bathroom, checked my email, refilled my coffee, sent a text message, and even clipped my toenails. *How did I get so distracted?!*

Unfortunately, what happened that morning isn't rare for me. If I'm not careful, this becomes my daily routine. Sometimes quieting my mind for prayer feels like giving a four-year-old boy ice cream and telling him to sit still. It's not going to happen!

Maybe you resonate with my struggle. It's no accident that Scripture commands clear and focused thinking when we pray. The apostle Peter admonishes us to "be self-controlled and sober-minded for the sake of your prayers" (1 Peter 4:7), and Paul adds

85

that we are to "continue steadfastly in prayer, being watchful in it" (Col. 4:2).

Even great heroes of the faith have struggled to focus while praying. C. S. Lewis once made this confession: "Incidentally, what most often interrupts my own prayers is not great distractions but tiny ones—things one will have to do or avoid in the course of the next hour."[1] Or consider this warning from Charles Spurgeon (which I'm guessing came from his own experience): "Permit not your minds to be easily distracted, or you will often have your devotion destroyed."[2]

While there is no silver-bullet answer to beating distraction and focusing when we pray, we can minimize the pull of what distracts us. First we need to understand why distraction is so destructive.

DISTRACTION IS WORSE THAN YOU THINK

Focus is essential in all areas of life—not only prayer. How would you like seeing your Uber driver reading a book while driving? Or maybe you'd prefer your surgeon to be sending texts during an operation? Obviously not. And yet we allow distractions to steal our attention—with results that are often subtler than a fender bender or a botched surgery.

"With the ever-present distractions in our lives, we are quickly becoming a people of shallow thoughts, and shallow thoughts will lead to shallow living," writes blogger and author Tim Challies. "There is a simple and inevitable progression at work here: Distraction —> Shallow Thinking —> Shallow Living."[3]

---

1. C. S. Lewis, *Letters to an American Lady*, ed. Clyde S. Kilby (repr., San Francisco: HarperOne, 2014), 73.

2. C. H. Spurgeon, *The Sword and Trowell: 1878* (London: Passmore & Alabaster, 1878), 136, quoted in Tony Reinke, *12 Ways Your Phone Is Changing You* (Wheaton, IL: Crossway, 2017), 128.

3. Tim Challies, *The Next Story: Life and Faith after the Digital Explosion* (Grand Rapids: Zondervan, 2011), 117.

While many people claim they don't want shallow lives, allowing constant distractions to creep into their lives betrays this claim. Tim Wu, author of the book *The Attention Merchants*, shares this sober warning: "When we reach the end of our days, our life experience will equal what we have paid attention to, whether by choice or by default."[4] While that may be an overstatement for believers (because we can't forget grace!), you get his point. We will one day face judgment for what we have done with the time and talents God has entrusted to us.

Perhaps the worst effect of letting distraction derail our prayers is the message it sends to God: *my trivial thoughts and anxieties are more important than You are.* God doesn't appreciate your half-hearted attention any more than my wife enjoys knowing I'm paying more attention to the TV than to her during an important conversation. Let us resolve to honor Him by disciplining our minds to pray faithfully.

WHY ARE WE SO DISTRACTED?

Since a proper treatment requires a proper diagnosis, let's look into why it is so easy for us to be distracted. Let me offer six suggestions.

1. We Have Competing Desires

Desires drive our lives, whether we realize it or not. When your mind wanders to your to-do list, your hobbies, your anxieties, or something else instead of focusing on God while you are praying, your desire for those other things overrides your desire for God.

The fear of missing out (which is abbreviated as *FOMO*) stirs up desires in us to be cool, to keep up with the Joneses, or to be

4. Tim Wu attributes this observation to William James in *The Attention Merchants: The Epic Scramble to Get Inside Our Heads* (New York: Alfred A. Knopf, 2016), 7.

in the loop with the latest news out there. When you are praying, FOMO might whisper to you that checking what's new on
social media or your favorite website is better than connecting
with God. It might cause you to overload your schedule, to the
detriment of your prayer time, because there are simply too many
exciting opportunities to pass up.

The only thing we should fear missing out on is God's will for
our lives. Our world is flooded with information, opportunities,
and the "next big thing"—which will be yesterday's news in a few
months (or sooner). Our lives are as they should be only when
God is our greatest desire (see Pss. 37:4; 73:25–26).

2. We Never Focus on Focusing

Many of us haven't actively diagnosed our lack of focus and
haven't sought to grow. The ability to focus is like a muscle that
can be strengthened over time. Have you ever exercised it? You'd
be surprised how productive it is to spend fifteen minutes thinking through your common distractions and how you can fight
them. The next section of this chapter will give you practical suggestions to help you to grow in your ability to focus.

3. The Pressures of Life Weigh upon Us

You have work to do, bills to pay, and family to look after.
You have a car that needs repair and a relationship that does, too.
Maybe you bring burdens home from work with you as well. All
of these pressures can make focusing a challenge. (And, unfortunately, they can choke out faith as well—see Mark 4:18–19).

4. We Are Lazy

Maybe you put off dull tasks until a time when you feel more
like doing them, but that time never seems to come. Do you avoid
important things because you don't want to exert mental energy
on a hard task or decision? That's called laziness, my friend. And

when you add up wasted chunks of time over several decades, it amounts to . . . well, something we will probably want to put off thinking about.

5. Using Technology Conditions Us to Be Distracted

Technology used to feel like a neutral tool. However, it's becoming clear that tech giants will use any means of enticement to keep you constantly using their products so they can gather data on you and then sell it.[5]

And not only do we have outside forces vying for our attention, but we also battle internally with sinful hearts that *enjoy* distraction. Studies show that the typical person checks his or her phone every twelve minutes—about eighty times per day.[6] When our phones aren't physically near us, we feel separation anxiety. A phone has become almost an additional appendage of the human body, which transforms us into distraction addicts. (Go ahead; see if you can go an hour without thinking about your phone.)

Have you seen the viral video of the girl who fell into a fountain at a mall because she was texting as she walked? Me too. And I'll admit I chuckled. But digital distraction has a dark side, too. Think of all the people who die because of car accidents that are caused by texting and driving. Or think of the kids who are injured because their parents were paying more attention to their phones than to the kids' safety (which is unfortunately a documented phenomenon[7]).

5. See Cal Newport, "A Lopsided Arms Race," chap. 1 in *Digital Minimalism: Choosing a Focused Life in a Noisy World* (New York: Portfolio, 2019).

6. See SWNS, "Americans Check Their Phones 80 Times a Day: Study," *New York Post*, November 8, 2017, https://nypost.com/2017/11/08/americans-check-their-phones-80-times-a-day-study/.

7. See Erika Christakis, "The Dangers of Distracted Parenting," *The Atlantic*, July/August 2018, https://www.theatlantic.com/magazine/archive/2018/07/the-dangers-of-distracted-parenting/561752/.

Don't hear me wrong—I'm not saying that being distracted from or during prayer equals homicide or child abuse. My point is that negative *physical* effects of technological distraction are a lot easier to spot than negative *spiritual* effects. For that reason, we need to maximize the benefits we get from technology and mitigate the aspects of it that hinder our relationship with God. (More on this later.)

6. We Can Lose the Ability to Focus

We may struggle to focus while praying simply because our bodies and minds can't focus like they used to. Scripture tells us our mortal bodies are wasting away (see 2 Cor. 4:16)—which may result from illness or simply aging. While overcoming physical weakness will always be a challenge for us, we can rest in the words of Psalm 73:26: "My flesh and my heart may fail, but God is the strength of my heart and my portion forever."

IMPROVING OUR FOCUS

Now that we've covered key reasons why it's tough for us to focus on or during prayer, I'm going to fill your toolbox with practical ways to grow in your ability to focus on praying.

1. Turn Your Attention from Distractions to God

The greatest thing we can do to improve our focus when we pray is to dwell on the person of God. Puritan Thomas Brooks gave this advice when he wrote about battling distraction during worship: "Oh! let your souls be greatly affected with the presence, purity, and majesty of that God before whom you stand. A man would be afraid of playing with a feather, when he is speaking with a king. . . . There is nothing that will contribute so much to the keeping out of vain thoughts, as to look upon God as an omniscient God, an omnipresent God, an omnipotent God, a God full of all glorious perfections."[8] When we set our minds and hearts on the glory and holiness of our God, our random thoughts melt in the heat of His majesty. Set your mind on God by meditating on a truth from Scripture, remembering His glorious works all throughout world history, and considering the fact that this God invites you to commune with Him through prayer.

Part of setting our minds on God involves hating whatever distraction enters our minds and resolving all the more to seek Him. Vain thoughts "pass through the best hearts," writes Brooks, but "they are lodged and cherished only in the worst hearts."[9]

2. Diagnose Sources of Your Distraction to Prevent Future Distraction

Distracting thoughts feel like gnats buzzing around my head. Swatting them with a flyswatter is necessary—but so is preventing their arrival in the first place. Think back through the last couple of weeks. In what way has distraction hindered your prayer time? What has distracted you? Some distractions you can't always help, but many you can. What do you fill your mind with—and have any of these things made it more difficult to focus on God while you are praying?

I'll give you a glimpse into my battle for focus against distraction. When I check my phone notifications first thing in the morning, it's that much harder for me to focus on seeking God through Scripture reading and prayer. My focus also suffers when I fill my mind with too much digital noise by listening to podcasts and audiobooks nonstop. Intentionally disciplining my entertainment intake has paid dividends for my focus in prayer.

8. Thomas Brooks, *Precious Remedies against Satan's Devices* (1652; repr., Carlisle, PA: Banner of Truth, 2011), 135. See also Kevin Halloran, "How to Fight Distraction in Worship: Wisdom from Thomas Brooks," *Anchored in Christ* (blog), September 4, 2018, https://www.kevinhalloran.net/how-to-fight-distraction-in-worship/.
9. Brooks, *Precious Remedies*, 137.

Other ways that you can prevent distraction are to build quiet into your life and set aside time to think. Limit your media intake. Turn off your phone for a few hours (or longer). Avoid multitasking—which decreases both your focus and your IQ.[10]

3. Follow a Path during Prayer

Chapter 2 lays out several paths you can take while praying that will keep you from falling into the ditch of distraction: praying prayers from Scripture, praying in response to your Bible reading, praying written prayers, or structuring your prayers around the petitions of the Lord's Prayer or the acronym ACTS. It's easier to follow a proven guide than to bushwhack your way through the wilderness. I will share a few more methods in the next chapter.

4. Write Down Your Prayers

A journal, word processor, or piece of paper are all you need to scribble down your prayers to God. This practice helps visual learners, like me, because it keeps our prayers always before us. An added advantage of writing down your prayers is that it enables you to review past prayers and see how God has answered them and you have grown.

5. Optimize Your Technology Use

Here's a commonsense tip: when it comes to technology, do whatever helps you to pray and fight whatever hinders you. My phone is a great source of distraction; but if I put it on airplane mode when it is time for me to pray, it removes the temptation for me to launch apps or check messages. I have also chosen not to use social media on my phone, due to its constant lure of trivial

---

10. See Geoffrey James, "Sitting Near a Multitasker Decreases Your Intelligence by 17 Percent," *Inc*, August 24, 2018, https://www.inc.com/geoffrey-james/multitasking -reduces-your-intelligence-by-17.html.

distractions. When it comes time for the spiritual disciplines of reading the Word and praying, I use a physical Bible and run an app that shuts off access to most of my other apps. Find what works for you, and do it!

6. Harness the Power of Routine

Dr. David Murray shares how a mentor of his had a special chair he would always use for morning devotions. This mentor had tried to focus at his work desk, but his mind would always drift to work, which prompted him to choose a different chair in order to aid his focus. By establishing a routine at his special "devotions chair," he trained his mind to be ready for spiritual pursuits as soon as he sat down. Routines like these are ideal for the establishing of habits.[11] What routine might you implement?

7. Pray When Your Mind Is Fresh

When do you have the most mental energy? If you're a morning person, like me, you are freshest after your morning coffee; and by the end of the day your brain feels like mush. Maybe you're a night owl and do your best thinking after others go to bed. Whatever your situation, plan your times of prayer for when it's easiest for you to focus. Our Father is worthy of receiving the firstfruits of our mental energy!

8. Take a Walk

When I realized that I focus better in prayer while I am going for a walk (or pacing in my house), I felt a new freedom. Adam and Eve walked and talked with God in the garden—why can't we where we are, as well?

My practice is to write Scriptures and requests on a note-card and refer to it as I walk. Walking takes me away from many

11. David Murray, "My Personal Devotions Chair," *HeadHeartHand* (blog), January 15, 2019, http://headhearthand.org/blog/2019/01/15/my-personal-devotions-chair/.

distractions, and my notecard gives me the structure I need to have a profitable prayer time.

9. Sing

If singing helps you to pray, then sing. Singing to God is praying with a tune. And what a difference it makes in warming your soul to draw near to the throne of grace! John Calvin recommended singing if it stirred "a true zeal and eagerness to pray." Though his recommendation came with an important caveat: "Yet we should be very careful that our ears be not more attentive to the melody than our minds to the spiritual meaning of the words."[12]

10. Set a Timer

Deadlines help me to focus when I am working—why not when I am praying? If I know that a timer will go off in twenty minutes, I'm more ready to focus on my prayer. Often, when the timer sounds, I add more time—because I have been able to warm up and am enjoying time with God.

11. Block Off Outside Distractions Using Earplugs or Headphones

Even when I don't have music on, the tactile stimulus of earplugs in my ear reminds me I have something important to do!

12. Consume Caffeine Wisely

Laugh all you want, but strong coffee greatly helps my ability to focus when I am praying!

13. Don't Give Up Too Early

Have you ever noticed that a good conversation with a friend or relative isn't automatic? Even if you're with your best friend,

12. *Calvin: Institutes of the Christian Religion*, vol. 2, *Books III.XX to IV.XX*, ed. John T. McNeill, trans. Ford Lewis Battles (Philadelphia: The Westminster Press, 1960), 3.20.32.

you can still fumble for good questions to ask or topics to talk about. After a while, however, your conversation warms up and you can talk about anything. Have you ever experienced that in your conversations with God?

The Puritans recommended "praying until you pray." D. A. Carson explains:

> What they mean is that Christians should pray long enough and honestly enough, at a single session, to get past the feeling of formalism and unreality that attends not a little praying. We are especially prone to such feelings when we pray for only a few minutes, rushing to be done with a mere duty. To enter the spirit of prayer, we must stick to it for a while. If we "pray until we pray," eventually we come to delight in God's presence, to rest in his love, to cherish his will. . . . In short, we discover a little of what Jude means when he exhorts his readers to "pray in the Holy Spirit" (Jude 20).[13]

It takes time to rev the engines of prayer. Keep at it, and focus will often come to you—even by supernatural means.

KEEP AT IT

I wish I could say that what I've presented in this chapter has cured my lack of focus forever—but that would be a lie. Yes, focusing when I'm praying is still a struggle for me, but I have found the tools that this chapter presents to be invaluable for helping me to resist distractions and come attentively to God.

The attitude that God wants us to have when we pray is reflected in a powerful image from Psalm 131: "I have calmed

13. D. A. Carson, *A Call to Spiritual Reformation: Priorities from Paul and His Prayers* (Grand Rapids: Baker Academic, 1992), 36.

and quieted my soul, like a weaned child with its mother; like a weaned child is my soul within me" (v. 2). A weaned child no longer approaches its mother solely for milk; a weaned child is there to enjoy its mother's presence. Calming our hearts in order to spend time with God has never been more important than now, when our world grows noisier and more distracting by the day. But with conscious effort and a growing love for God, we will grow in focus—and we will pray.

PRAYER

Dear heavenly Father, my mind is weak and I often love the trivial. Lift my eyes from trivialities to be able to see You in Your glory. Help me to strengthen my self-control, in every area of life, so I can serve You and love others better. Show me what will help me to stay focused the most while I am seeking You in prayer. In Jesus's name, amen.

QUESTIONS FOR REFLECTION

1. Where does your mind run when you are trying to pray? What practices might you take from this chapter to discipline your mind for more serious thought?
2. What circumstances make focusing when you pray easy for you? Hard?
3. What sins do you need to confess regarding the ways you are distracted?
4. Which of the practical ways of focusing that this chapter has presented will you try to implement? Is there any other practice that helps you to focus while you are praying?

7

i'm so unorganized

*"[Pray] at all times in the Spirit, with all prayer and supplication.
To that end, keep alert with all perseverance, making supplication
for all the saints." —Paul the apostle, Ephesians 6:18*

Imagine receiving a call from the president in which you are told
that he (or she) would like to meet for an hour next week in order
for you to affect nationwide policy. What would it look like for you
to take such a meeting seriously? You'd probably maximize the
opportunity by praying about it, consulting wise friends, reading
as much as you could, and planning details for your time together.
What if I told you that someone who was given the same opportunity instead winged it and shared only what was on the top of
his mind? That would be a waste of a great opportunity, right?

Many of us approach prayer that way. We have a moment-by-
moment invitation from the all-powerful Creator of the universe
to present our petitions, for ourselves and on behalf of others,
before him. And we often take that invitation for granted. Our
nonchalant attitude reveals that we have an anemic view of prayer
and of the God we pray to.

This chapter is all about how to intentionally take advantage of the gift of prayer. God invites us to pray because He *wants* to answer and work through our prayers—why not take advantage of this invitation? I'll admit I was tempted not to include this chapter in the book, because I thought it would be too straightforward and tedious. I have since changed my mind. I now think that *this may be the chapter that will bear the most eternal fruit.* Why?

Think about the law of compound interest. The law states that the more money we invest up front, the more it will grow over time. The interest we earn in the early years of investing will add to our initial investment and cause the interest we earn in later years to be much greater. It's the snowball effect. And I think this applies to our prayers as well. As we organize our prayers and petitions and faithfully bring them to God over the long term, He answers them, and the fruit that is borne from these answers to prayer can multiply. God may answer our prayer for the salvation of a friend, and over the next few years that friend may lead others to Christ. God may answer our prayer for our pastor to be spiritually strengthened, and his ministry may bear much fruit as a result. By faithfully praying over the long haul for everything that God wants us to pray for, we will bear much fruit.

The goal of organizing our prayers is to take the commands God gives us in Scripture as seriously as possible by obeying them as intentionally as possible. By doing so, we invest more of our lives in the kingdom of God.

WHO SHOULD WE PRAY FOR?

This is a companion chapter to chapter 2. Whereas chapter 2 offered broad guidance on the content of our prayers, this chapter will help us to think through specific requests and intercessions that God wants us to make. It will also introduce a few simple methods for how you can organize many different prayer priorities and requests—because, if you're like me, you can't remember them all without writing them down. The methods will also keep us from getting stuck, while we're praying, on the same requests and petitions that often focus on our little worlds. God wants to impact everything that is listed below through your prayers. Praying for these things isn't optional—they are priorities that flow from the commands of Scripture and, thus, from the heart of God. The following section on methods *is* optional, but it's worth thinking through.

As we think about organizing our prayers, let me remind you of the utmost importance of praying with scriptural priorities. We pray effectively when we pray what God wants us to pray—we can pray as a direct response to Scripture or can let scriptural truth inform what we pray about (see chapter 2). Praying with scriptural priorities means that we don't neglect spiritual and eternal needs by focusing only on temporal needs—so, yes, we should pray for physical health and healing, but we should prioritize salvation and spiritual growth. We organize our prayers, in large part, so that we can address the topics and needs that matter most to God.

Ourselves

How should we pray for ourselves? We know our lives, our needs, our struggles, our deficiencies, and our blind spots better than anyone—except God. Let's pray for spiritual growth, spiritual strength, God's wisdom to help us love others well, and God's power to help us be faithful witnesses for Jesus to our lost world.

Friends and Family

It makes sense for us to pray for those we love the most. Pray for their salvation, spiritual growth, guidance, provision, and protection.

Governmental Officials

Who are the local, regional, national, and international government officials you can pray for? You don't have to like a politician to pray for them! Pray for them to be saved and for their work to result in freedom for the gospel to advance and in peaceful, quiet, and dignified lives for us (see 1 Tim. 2:1–6). I fully expect to see many of today's earthly rulers in heaven, worshipping the King of Kings with joyful and repentant hearts (see Ps. 2:10–12). After all, why would God command us to pray for the salvation of kings and authorities if He didn't plan to save some?

Your Enemies

Jesus's countercultural command "Love your enemies and pray for those who persecute you" (Matt. 5:44) reminds us of the goodness and transforming power of His gospel. He is still transforming the lives of His enemies today—just as He did for the apostle Paul so many years ago. If you can't think of any personal enemies that you have, first, thank God—and then consider the many people in the world who are ideologically opposed to the gospel of Jesus, and pray for them.

All People

God calls us to pray for all kinds of people (see Eph. 6:18). What specific people do you know who may not have believers in their lives who are praying for them? Who does the Lord bring to your mind at random times? What groups of people are affected by major events in the news, by great injustices, or by cultural issues that weigh heavy on your heart? Pray for these people.

The Local Church

Lift up your local congregation. Pray for the spiritual vitality of your pastors and elders and of their families. Pray for your small group, the sick, missionary partners around the world, and your church's witness in its community. Pray for God to work in and through other churches that are in your community. Consider asking a pastor for a list of prayer requests, and for the names of the members of your church, so you can pray for them.

The Global Church

Pray for the advancement of the gospel around the world.[1] Pray for persecuted Christians.[2] Pray for the Lord to send more laborers into His harvest (see Matt. 9:37–38). Pray for Christian organizations and institutions—many of which will even send out prayer guides that you can follow. Pray for God's glory to cover the earth as the waters cover the sea (see Hab. 2:14).

A FEW RECOMMENDED METHODS
FOR ORGANIZING PRAYERS

Implementing one or more of the following organization methods *is* optional but still well worth thinking through. The methods are simple (which is hopefully a relief to you!), but they may be exactly what you need in order to break free from organizational struggles as you pray. Megan Hill knows a lot about prayer as a pastor's wife, a mother of four, an editor for a large evangelical website, and an author of a book on prayer.[3] That's what makes her confession so intriguing: "The thing that's been most helpful to me in my personal prayer life *is to be organized*."[4]

1. Two invaluable resources for praying for the global church are Jason Mandryk, *Operation World: The Definitive Prayer Guide to Every Nation*, 7th ed. (repr., Downers Grove, IL: IVP Books, 2010) and Molly Wall, advising ed., *Pray for the World: A New Prayer Resource from Operation World* (Downers Grove, IL: IVP Books, 2015).

2. Voice of the Martyrs (https://www.persecution.com/) and Open Doors (https://www.opendoors.org/) are two organizations that can help you to do this.

3. See Megan Hill, *Praying Together: The Priority and Privilege of Prayer; In Our Homes, Communities, and Churches* (Wheaton, IL: Crossway, 2016).

4. Megan Hill, "Megan Hill on Most Helpful Practices for Personal Prayer," The Gospel Coalition, May 13, 2017, video, 2:56, https://www.thegospelcoalition.org/article

Before we dig into the recommended methods of organization, let's quickly consider three potential dangers of using these methods:

- *Legalism.* A method can easily turn into a routine that we follow in order to earn God's approval. These methods are helpful *tools*, not binding *rules*. If they help you, great! If they don't, set them aside. God accepts you because of Jesus, not because you're a beast at following a method.
- *Mechanical prayers.* Done wrongly, a method for prayer becomes hoops for us to jump through—which changes the goal of prayer from knowing and honoring God to simply finishing a routine. Don't forget that God wants your heart.
- *Shallow prayers.* If we try to pray for too many petitions at once, our prayers merely skip across the surface like a rock on a lake. (That's why I'll recommend cycling through a wide variety of requests on a weekly or monthly basis.)

Method 1: Keep a Prayer List

This idea is simple: get something to write on (a journal, loose-leaf paper, or a digital document), write down a list of prayer requests as well as Scriptures to pray, and pray through that list regularly. Writing lists keeps you focused and allows you to see how God has worked in your life over time. Theologian D. A. Carson keeps a folder for prayer that has several sheets of paper inside.[5] After dating each entry, he lists long-term prayer requests along with relevant Scriptures in a column on the left side of a sheet and saves room on the right side for recording answers to those prayers. He uses another sheet for short- or intermediate-range

/megan-hill-on-most-helpful-practices-for-personal-prayer/, emphasis added.

5. Read more about his method in D. A. Carson, *A Call to Spiritual Reformation: Priorities from Paul and His Prayers* (Grand Rapids: Baker Academic, 1992), 27–29.

concerns (related to either his family or ministry) and regularly adds or deletes content, as needed, to keep that page up to date. His folder also contains an assortment of letters and notes from others whom he'd like to keep in prayer. Dr. Donald Whitney prefers a loose-leaf paper approach, because he can take it with him easily (often by stuffing it into his Bible) and organize it into a larger body of journal entries.[6]

Method 2: Use Index Cards

Paul E. Miller popularized the use of index cards for prayer in his book *A Praying Life*.[7] Miller writes a person ("My Wife") or category ("My Work" or "People in Suffering") on a 3x5" index card, adds a verse or two he would like to pray regarding each person or category, and shares a few petitions about said person or category. Miller prefers this card system because he's able to focus on one card at a time better then staring at a huge list.[8] He prays through several cards a day—some of them every day and others at different frequencies. He outlines what a deck of prayer cards might consist of:

- 4–10 cards for individual family members
- 1–3 cards for people who are suffering
- 1 card for friends
- 1 card for non-Christians
- 1 card for church leadership
- 1 card for his small group
- 1 card for missionaries or ministries
- 1–3 cards for world or cultural issues

6. See Donald S. Whitney, *Spiritual Disciplines for the Christian Life*, rev. and updated ed. (Colorado Springs: NavPress, 2014), 267.

7. See Paul E. Miller, "Keeping Track of the Story: Using Prayer Cards," chap. 29 in *A Praying Life: Connecting with God in a Distracting World*, rev. ed. (Colorado Springs: NavPress, 2017).

8. See Miller, 230.

- 3 cards for work-related issues
- 1 card for coworkers
- 3–5 cards for things he needs to repent of
- 3–5 cards for hopes or big dreams[9]

I use a digital prayer-card method with the help of an app on my phone. The app that I use, PrayerMate, organizes various lists of prayer requests into larger categories, allowing me to incorporate diverse prayer requests, on a variety of topics, into my prayers. I start off with a scriptural prayer (from a collection of several dozen) to prime the pump of my heart with truth. My next category contains four prayer cards—each of which targets a specific element of my walk with God: (1) delight in God and His Word, (2) my identity in Christ, (3) the fear of God, and (4) hating sin. I then move through several other categories, each containing prayer cards filled with various Scriptures and petitions. I can customize each digital card based on how often I want to pray for it (daily, weekly, monthly, and so on). If I don't customize this frequency, the cards by default will rotate, ensuring that I eventually work through every card on my list. I even have a "Random" category for the requests that don't have a logical place. I love this method and don't think I'll ever switch. It's too convenient to always have with me (especially while I'm traveling) and too helpful for organizing a boatload of requests. (The obvious downside of it is that it's on the most distracting device in the universe!)

Method 3: Pray in Concentric Circles

Pastor John Piper recommends a method that begins with imagining yourself standing in the middle of several concentric circles.[10] Each circle represents a category of people. After praying

9. See Miller, 236.
10. See John Piper, "Devote Yourselves to Prayer," Desiring God, January 9, 2000, https://www.desiringgod.org/messages/devote-yourselves-to-prayer.

for yourself (the first circle), you move to the subsequent circles by praying for your family, then your church, then your work, then your community, and so on—until you get to a global circle.

Method 4: Designate Categories for Every Day of the Week

My friend Brandon and his wife Kaiti have a different focus for each day of the week when they pray together. It's a strategy you could use for your personal prayer.

Sunday	Pray for the week ahead
Monday	Pray for their immediate and extended family
Tuesday	Pray for their nation and the world (churches, government leaders, current events, and so on)
Wednesday	Pray for their friends, neighbors, and local church
Thursday	Pray for their marriage[11]
Friday	Offer specific praise and thanksgiving
Saturday	Pray for the gathering of God's people on Sunday—and specifically for them to be unified in the gospel, for the global church to expand, and for God to be glorified

Method 5: Create Your Own Approach

The key to any approach is that *it work for you*. You could cobble together your own approach using elements of the four methods above, or you could adopt one of those approaches and use it for the rest of your life.

My friend D'Andre has his own approach. He has a five-column spreadsheet for people he's praying for that contains a column for each category that the people belong to: high school,

11. They also use this day as a time to check in with each other.

college, work, and so on. He normally prays for one column per day and rotates through them. He also has a general prayer request document that he updates regularly by cycling in new requests and removing short-term requests as he prays for them.

Some people may have such sharp memories that using a system would get in their way—though I suspect that these people are few and far between. Don't worry about using a method every day or creating the "perfect prayer list." These methods are simply tools that you can use to pursue faithfulness out of love for God and your neighbor.

WHAT I DO

Each morning, after about twenty or twenty-five minutes of Bible reading (which often involves periods of meditation and prayer), I transition fully into prayer. Sometimes I grab my phone and spend ten or fifteen minutes cycling through the day's prayer cards on my PrayerMate app. Other times I walk through the petitions in the Lord's Prayer and add in specific praises and requests as I go.[12] I also tuck prayer guides from my church and from organizations that I support into my Bible. My wife and I follow a pattern together that's similar to method 4, and at meals we also sometimes pull an index card out of our "prayer box" and pray for its contents. I implement all of these methods for a very simple reason: they help me to pray!

A POTENTIAL OBJECTION

"But this is a lot of work!" some may protest.

Yes; implementing any of these methods is work. But so is buying groceries; so is raising kids; so is planning a vacation.

12. See chapter 2 for an example of how I pray for my marriage by following the Lord's Prayer.

Here is the real question: *Is it worth it?* I think we know the right answer.

Implementing a method doesn't have to be much work. If you spent five minutes right now working on organizing your future prayers using one of (or a combination of) these methods, and then incorporated more requests into that method as time goes on, I'm sure you'd pray for more things in the future than if you merely relied on your memory. A simple system goes a long way toward helping you to pray more faithfully.

IMAGINE THE FUTURE

What if God answered all your prayers for people to be saved? What if every prayer you offered about spiritual growth and protection for others was answered in ways beyond your wildest dreams? Would it cause you to pray differently? The fact is that God promises to use our prayers. We don't know exactly how; we don't know exactly when. Often the answers to our prayers go unseen, or we simply forget what we have prayed. Often God works out His purposes in His timing—which means we may die before knowing how He will fully answer. We'll never know the fruit of some of our prayers. Your prayers today for the salvation of a child might be answered tomorrow or a hundred years from now.

Praying for all kinds of people is like sowing seeds. We don't know when the seeds will germinate and cause a new plant to grow. We don't know when those plants will produce and release their own seeds. We don't know what will become of each seed. But just as one single seed could eventually produce an entire forest, one single prayer could change a life, a nation, or the course of human history.[13] The question is, what will you do about it?

13. For remarkable stories of how God has worked through prayer in the past, I recommend Collin Hansen and John Woodbridge, *A God-Sized Vision: Revival Stories That Stretch and Stir* (Grand Rapids: Zondervan, 2010).

PRAYER

Father, it is astounding to see the breadth of areas that You want us to pray about—and more astounding to realize that You want to effect change in these areas through us. Please help me to craft the right system that will allow me to take the gift of prayer and intercession as seriously as possible. And please deepen my desire to invest in eternity through the prayers I offer today. In Jesus's name, amen.

QUESTIONS FOR REFLECTION

1. Have you ever used a system or a method for organizing your prayer requests? If so, how has it helped you?
2. After reading this chapter, were you moved to dedicate more energy to praying for certain people or things that God commands? If so, what?
3. Which of this chapter's five organizational methods do you think will work best for you?
4. What change do you think could happen in the world if you took praying for others more seriously? Describe what the future might look like if you took this chapter to heart.

8

i'm too stressed

"What a friend we have in Jesus, all our sins and griefs to bear!
What a privilege to carry everything to God in prayer!
O what peace we often forfeit, O what needless pain we bear,
All because we do not carry everything to God in prayer!"
—Joseph Scriven, "What a Friend We Have in Jesus"

Year after year, search data from major Bible websites shows Philippians 4:6–7 to be one of the most popular passages in Scripture—and with good reason: it shows us God's proven path that will take us from anxiety to peace.[1] The passage reads,

> Do not be anxious about anything, but in everything by prayer and supplication with thanksgiving let your requests be made known to God. And the peace of God, which surpasses all understanding, will guard your hearts and your minds in Christ Jesus. (Phil. 4:6–7)

1. A portion of this chapter is based on an article I wrote. See Kevin Halloran, "When Prayer Makes Anxiety Worse," Unlocking the Bible, August 14, 2019, https://unlocking thebible.org/2019/08/when-prayer-makes-anxiety-worse/.

Unfortunately, our desperate hearts can easily get off track when we are seeking a remedy for our stress. We treat this precious passage as a lucky charm and miss its true meaning and the path to peace that it lays out. A recent situation of mine illustrates this.

As I was thinking through a stressful time at work, my anxiety about it worsened. When I tried to fix my attention on something else, the same thing happened—just when I thought I had escaped it, my anxiety boomeranged back. As I thought about how God might be wanting me to calm my heart, Philippians 4:6–7 came to mind. *Prayer to the rescue!*

So I knelt down to pray. My prayer started out fine—but soon I felt like I was trapped in a hot car, breathing the same stale air over and over. With each line of my prayer, I gasped for breath and became *more anxious.* I ended the prayer more anxious than when I had begun. What happened? What about God's promise of peace from Philippians 4:6–7? As I reflected on this troubling episode, I realized that the problem wasn't with God's promise— it was with me.

BATTLING SINFUL ANXIETY THROUGH PRAYER

Stress is a huge topic, and we won't be able to explore everything about it in this chapter. What we will focus on is *how we can avoid sinful anxiety while honoring God and experiencing His peace through prayer.* This chapter will take a different approach than others: it will help us to know how to think and pray during anxious times. We'll look at what I got wrong about Philippians 4 as well as how we can get it right and experience the peace of God that passes all understanding.

Before we dive in, let's define what we're talking about. *Anxiety* refers to "painful or apprehensive uneasiness of mind usu[ally] over an impending or anticipated ill" or a "fearful concern or interest."[2] Anxiety can be a gift from God—an alarm bell telling us that something's not right. If my young daughter darts into a busy street, anxiety propels me to grab her before she gets hurt. Anxiety because of a looming deadline might motivate a student to get off social media and finish an assignment. It becomes destructive, however, when we respond to it in sinful ways. When this happens, we may shift our focus from honoring God to pleasing ourselves. We may become self-reliant when we realize that God isn't acting in the way we want. Because He isn't taking away our burden with the snap of His fingers, we decide to bear it ourselves.[3]

Anxiety exists on a spectrum ranging from normal, everyday fears to extreme disorders and panic attacks. Its causes range from everyday stressors to traumatic events to biological imbalances.[4] There may even be spiritual forces behind your anxiety, since the Enemy of our souls loves to see God's children stress. This chapter will focus on the everyday anxiety that we face. Yet the truth it unpacks from God's Word will help with more intense experiences as well, because no one, no matter the circumstances, can shortcut his or her spiritual duty of fighting a sinful response to anxiety through prayer.[5]

I'm no biblical counselor or anxiety expert, but I have battled it myself. A stressful time during seminary led me to experience heart palpitations and seek professional help. At other times, stress has led me to have days-long migraine headaches. Stressful seasons have left me drained of physical and emotional energy

2. *Merriam-Webster's Collegiate Dictionary*, 11th ed. (2003), s.v. "anxiety."

3. See Gary R. Collins, *Christian Counseling: A Comprehensive Guide*, 3rd ed. (Nashville: Nelson Reference & Electronic, 2007), 142.

4. See Collins, 143–48.

5. If you're concerned about your stress levels, first evaluate your basic self-care habits—whether you are getting proper sleep, eating healthy, and exercising. If you find that your stress levels are beyond your control and what is normal, seek help by talking to your pastor or finding a Christian counselor who can help you.

and apathetic about important people and responsibilities in my life. The truth that I share in this chapter is battle-tested.

HOW (NOT) TO PRAY WHEN YOU'RE REALLY STRESSED OUT

Anxiety ties us in knots, and pursuing quick fixes for it often tightens these knots instead of bringing relief. That's why I encourage you to slow down, analyze your thoughts, and dig deep into your heart in order to untangle the underlying issues of your anxiety. We can allow the challenges of life to push us further into despair, or we can channel them, like a sail catches a gust of wind, to propel us to greater humility and joyful dependence on the Lord.

After I realized that praying was making my anxiety worse, I conducted a postmortem analysis of what had happened—which revealed that my prayers were masking a sinful and struggling heart. God doesn't promise that any type of prayer will be a silver-bullet anxiety stopper. The *content* of our prayers matters. The *motives of our hearts* matter. We don't get points just for trying. As we learned in chapter 2, we need to align our prayers with scriptural truth. If we don't, we will feel like I did during my anxious episode—like we're stuck in a hot car breathing in the stale air of anxious thoughts and emotions. By praying the way God wants us to, we roll down the windows and let in fresh air. And we experience peace. The rest of this chapter will focus on six God-given mind-shifts we can make in order to fight anxiety through prayer.

Don't Pray to a Magic Genie; Pray to Your Father in Heaven

Remembering who you are praying to is just as important as the words of your prayers, because your view of God shapes your prayers and molds your heart—for better or for worse. Thinking of God as a wish-granting genie who will take away your worry with a snap of his fingers might make you *more* anxious when you realize that He doesn't work on your timetable!

Instead, remember God as Father. No good earthly father wants to see his children distressed, and every good father wants to help to bear his children's burdens. Good fathers also know what is best for their children. Our heavenly Father invites us to unload our anxieties before Him—and He is fully able to carry them.

Australian pastor Ray Galea has shared about a counselor he knows who requires all her new Christian clients to spend twenty minutes each day talking to their heavenly Father about their anxieties before they come to their first counseling session. The counselor has reported that the mere act of talking to their heavenly Father about their concerns has led many people to cancel their appointments. Why? Because by doing so, they have found what they needed more than an earthly counselor: the Wonderful Counselor, who cares for His children and has all the power in the universe to work in their lives and situations.[6]

Don't Be Prideful and Self-Centered; Be Humble and God-Centered

Our world and our technological devices tell us that we are at the center of our lives. And, in our sinful pride, we often believe them! But your life isn't about you. All things were created *by* Jesus and *for* Jesus (see Col. 1:16). The sin of pride leads us to overvalue ourselves and undervalue our sovereign Creator. The mindset that this puts us in fuels anxiety, instead of removing it, and often invites other nasty sins such as grumbling, cynicism, coveting, entitlement, and, ultimately, unbelief.

---

6. See Ray Galea, *From Here to Eternity: Assurance in the Face of Sin and Suffering* (Youngstown: Matthias Media, 2017), chap. 6, Kindle. Don't take this to mean that we don't need godly and gifted earthly counselors! My point is *not* that we shouldn't seek human counselors; it's that we should seek our heavenly Counselor first.

As I think back to my anxious situation, I now realize that I was lacking humility. My mouth was saying the right words, but my heart was praying the wrong ones: "God, come on—You owe me one. I deserve better!"

We need humility in order to step out of the fog of pride-induced anxiety and onto the path of peace. That's why Peter writes, in 1 Peter 5:6–7, "Humble yourselves, therefore, under the mighty hand of God so that at the proper time he may exalt you, *casting all your anxieties on him.*" When we bow before God in humility, when we admit our inability and recognize His ability, and when we offer Him our burdens, He takes them. Why? Because He cares for us (see v. 7). When we don't cast our anxieties on Him, we hold on to them ourselves instead.

To cultivate God-centered humility, ask Him for the grace to see your circumstances from His perfect perspective. Ask Him for the wisdom to be able to process the external details of your anxiety. Ask Him to reveal sin and wrong thinking in your heart. As you humble yourself before your loving Father this way, the tangled mess of your anxiety will begin to unravel.

Don't Be Indifferent or Angry; Be Thankful

Paul doesn't prescribe any type of prayer in Philippians 4; instead, he says that the prayers we do pray should involve "supplication with thanksgiving" (v. 6). A heart that lacks gratitude will not experience the peace of God. The self-centered pity party I described having earlier proved to be the *opposite* of thankfulness. A thankful heart isn't only a remedy for anxiety; it's part of a healthy spiritual diet for every circumstance (see 1 Thess. 5:16–18) as well as an essential part of spiritual warfare—because "the enemy's hold on [us] is loosened when we learn to be grateful to God."[7]

7. H. B. Charles Jr., "Warfare Prayer" (sermon, Shiloh Metropolitan Baptist Church, Jacksonville, FL, July 11, 2016).

Giving thanks *in everything* includes doing so in even the most frustrating situations. In fact, the power of giving thanks is often *most* potent in challenging times. Consider what is said to have been the reaction of the Puritan Matthew Henry when he had his wallet stolen: "I am thankful that he never robbed me before. I am thankful that although he took my wallet, he did not take my life. Although he took all I had, it was not much. I am glad that it was I who was robbed, not I who did the robbing."[8] Do you see what happened? Henry's gratitude turned a terrible situation into a worshipful experience. That's the power of gratitude!

My go-to practice for expelling anxious thoughts through thanksgiving is journaling. If I don't write down my thankful thoughts, I often forget them immediately. When I do write them down, I have a growing mountain of evidence of how good God has been to me and of how my situation isn't as bad as I think. After compiling my list of what I can be thankful for, I pore over it in prayer and give thanks to God. When my mind strays and starts digging another hole of self-centered negativity, I turn back to my list. Each reason for thankfulness on it serves as a rung of a ladder that helps me out of the pit.

I learned to journal about thankfulness from my mom. She was a wise and godly woman who served as a nurse for decades. She began thankfulness journaling while she battled the cancer that eventually took her life. My mom's prior medical experience became both a blessing and a curse during her battle with cancer; sometimes it helped her to get new nurses up to speed with what medicine she needed, and other times it gave her the real scoop on a prognosis that a doctor tried to sugarcoat. Her thankfulness journal served as a buoy in stormy waters that kept her from sinking into despair.

---

8. This account, which can be found in different versions in many places, may be apocryphal, but the lesson remains powerful.

She has since gone to be with the Lord; and while I don't know whether her journal still exists, here are a few things that I know she gave thanks for: *I'm thankful God saved me from my sin in my twenties. I'm thankful for a loving husband, believing children, and a church that loves God's Word. I'm thankful that I can be a witness for Jesus to other ladies receiving chemotherapy who don't have eternal hope. I'm thankful that neither death nor life nor powers nor anything else in all of creation—including cancer—can separate me from the love of God in Christ Jesus.*

The beauty of being in Christ is that we never face a hopeless circumstance or a lack of things for us to give thanks for. We can (and should!) thank Him for our salvation, for our adoption into His family, for providing all our needs. Even when a situation seems bleak, we can *always* be 100 percent certain that God will work all things for the good of those who love Him (see Rom. 8:28).

It's only through thanksgiving that we get to the place that Philippians 4:7 describes, where "the peace of God, which surpasses all understanding, will guard [our] hearts and [our] minds in Christ Jesus." The image Paul uses here is of a military garrison that is actively guarding the hearts and minds of those who pray. This peace is greater than you can imagine (it "surpasses all understanding") and is guarded by God Himself—meaning that it is stronger and more impenetrable than the greatest military fort in history. (Sorry, Fort Knox!) When you have this peace, no matter what happens, your heart and mind will be secure in Jesus. Now that's something to be thankful for!

Don't Meditate on Your Anxieties; Meditate on the Good

Maybe it's an annoying situation with a family member or coworker; maybe it's a troubling diagnosis or a frustrating conversation that you play over and over in your head. (And if you're like me, this leads you to come up with better arguments after the fact!) When we approach God in prayer while thinking only of these things, we pour gasoline on the fires of anxiety. What we are doing in this situation is leaning on our own understanding, which we're taught *not* to do (see Prov. 3:5–6)—and for a few reasons. First, it's the opposite of trusting in the Lord; and second, it presumes we have the ability to fully understand our situations— no matter how simple or complex they seem.

The only way for us to douse the fires of anxiety is to set our minds on the good stuff of Philippians 4:8: "Whatever is *true*, whatever is *honorable*, whatever is *just*, whatever is *pure*, whatever is *lovely*, whatever is *commendable*, if there is any *excellence*, if there is anything *worthy of praise*, think about these things."[9] And setting our minds on things like this isn't a one-time action (since the fires of anxiety can quickly return); it is a *continual* meditation.

We need an approach to meditating on the good that is both defensive and offensive. We must block (to the degree that we can) influences in our lives that fill our minds with fear and anxiety. For some people, that will mean taking a fast from political news or social media. Other people may realize that certain relationships are fueling their anxiety and should think of ways to minimize the harmful influence of those relationships. Meditating on good things during my own anxious situation forced me to look beyond my immediate frustrations to greater realities that were underlying my life. I found that I would not have had frustrations in the first place if it weren't for all the blessings God had lavished upon me! An alternative way to focus on the good is to ask yourself, "What is the worst that could happen in this situation?" Typically, an answer to this question will de-escalate unreasonable anxiety and produce gratitude.

I asked a counselor friend of mine what Bible passages he recommends for those who are struggling with anxiety, and his

9. A similar Scriptural idea is that of taking "every thought captive to obey Christ" (2 Cor. 10:5).

response surprised me at first: "Psalm 119." But then I quickly realized the wisdom of his recommendation—Psalm 119 is a lengthy meditation by the psalmist on his delight in God's Word and the reflection of its power in his life. When I read Psalm 119, the psalmist's words stir my affections for God and even help me to see the positive effects my anxiety can have if I submit it to the Lord: "It is good for me that I was afflicted, that I might learn your statutes" (v. 71).

When we are in Jesus, there is always an upside to our anxieties and suffering. Yet we can never be reminded of that if we don't focus on good things. It shouldn't surprise us to realize that God's Word reveals what is good in life better than anything else does. According to Psalm 19:7–11, His Word is *perfect, sure, right, pure, clean, true, more desirable than gold*, and *sweeter than honey*.

When anxiety leaves a bitter taste in your mouth, take hold of the Word of God as a weapon to use against it (see Heb. 4:12). When anxious thoughts flood your mind, dam them up by reciting Scripture. Sing worship music that proclaims biblical truth. Read the way that the psalmists battled anxiety through prayer, and make their prayers your own. You must fill your mind with something true and positive if you're going to escape the clutches of worry.

Don't Pray Alone; Pray alongside Believers, Past and Present

There are a couple of ways we can look to others for help in this area: first by reaching out to them when we need prayer, and second by looking to faithful examples of how we can persevere in prayer.

The Enemy of our souls wants you to think that you're all alone. He wants you to think that your friends and fellow church members are too busy for you or uninterested in helping you. (If that's true of your friends or church members, then pray for new ones!) But Scripture commands us to "bear one another's burdens" (Gal. 6:2). Who can you call to help lighten your load by praying for you?

We should also look to examples of the faithful to motivate us to persevere in our prayers. In Philippians 4:9, Paul holds out his own example as something that will help the Philippians to encounter God's peace: "What you have learned and received and heard and seen *in me*—practice these things, and the God of peace will be with you."

Paul is a stellar example of having faithful endurance during stressful times. He wrote the book of Philippians while he was in prison, and yet he could say, "I have learned in whatever situation I am to be content. I know how to be brought low, and I know how to abound. In any and every circumstance, I have learned the secret of facing plenty and hunger, abundance and need" (Phil. 4:11–12).

Paul's faithful example is worth pondering, as are other faithful examples in your life.[10] When my heart pulls me toward worry, I remember people like Farhad, who had to flee his home country of Iran after converting to Christianity.[11] I remember Corrie ten Boom, who faithfully endured life in a Nazi concentration camp during World War II.[12] I think of others at my church who have faithfully persevered while experiencing the hardship of losing a loved one, a job, or their health. I look to my Savior, who sweat drops of blood as he agonized over the suffering that awaited Him on the cross where he would die for our sin (see Matt. 26:36–46). I even look to *myself*—not as a stellar example, but because I

10. Peter makes this point after warning his readers to beware of the Enemy's influence: "Resist him, firm in your faith, knowing that the same kinds of suffering are being experienced by your brotherhood throughout the world" (1 Peter 5:9). You're not alone in the battle!

11. His name has been changed to protect his identity.

12. Read her story in Corrie ten Boom with John and Elizabeth Sherrill, *The Hiding Place: The Triumphant True Story of Corrie ten Boom* (1971; repr., New York: Bantam Books, 1974).

have a growing wealth of experiences of times when God proved Himself to be faithful throughout my challenges.[13]

Who can help you to battle anxiety, by praying for you or by providing an example that can spur you on to persevere in your prayer?

Don't Believe That God Has Abandoned You; Realize That He Is with You

My uncle and aunt experienced God's powerful presence while visiting a missionary couple in a poor Latin American country. On the last day of their trip, they decided to sightsee with these missionary friends. While driving to their destination, they saw a beautiful view and pulled over to take pictures. Before they knew it, three kidnappers ushered them back into their van at gunpoint. The kidnappers drove them to an abandoned farm that was miles away from civilization. An edifying ministry trip quickly turned into a real-life horror movie. *What will our kidnappers do to us? Did they bring us here to kill us? What will happen to our kids back home?* All they could do was pray. With guns pointed at their heads, the four removed all their jewelry and the money from their wallets for the kidnappers. And then the kidnappers fled.

"It was a time of feeling God's presence like never before," my aunt reflected afterward. "We all shared with each other, after the experience, that we all were in constant prayer and that God gave us His perfect peace. We also say that the minute we took our eyes off the Lord and put them on the circumstance, we had tremendous fear and anxiety!"

God is with us in the anxieties we feel in even the most intense

---

13. Other Scriptural examples of people who prayed through anxiety include Hannah (see 1 Sam. 1:1–2:11), King Hezekiah (see 2 Kings 20; Isa. 37–38), David in the Psalms (see the appendix for a list of suggested psalms), and the prophet Habakkuk throughout the book that bears his name.

of situations, like being kidnapped at gunpoint. That's why, in Philippians 4, Paul mentions not once, but twice, the promise of God's presence. He brackets the prescription for anxiety that he gives in Philippians 4:6–7 by saying "the Lord is at hand" (v. 5) and "practice these things [that he has been mentioning], and the God of peace will be with you" (v. 9). When we pray during anxiety the way God intends us to, we encounter the God of peace—as my uncle and aunt did.

God's presence not only gives us peace but also gives us a supernatural strength. When we feel that our burdens have doubled, we can trust that God can triple our strength.[14] Jeremiah Burroughs explains that, because of God's strengthening presence, "[our] burden will not be heavier, but lighter than it was before."[15] What incredible, divine help! This is exactly what Paul experienced, and it's why he could say triumphantly, even while in chains, "I can do all things through him who strengthens me" (Phil. 4:13). So can we.

AN AMAZING OPPORTUNITY

While I still battle anxiety from time to time, remembering these six ways of fighting anxiety through prayer has changed me. Anxiety no longer dominates my life and prayers; instead, it drives me to humbly pray to my loving Father, fix my mind on what is true and good, and remember that He is with me. I can more readily accept His promise of peace and set my heart on the One who transcends all my problems and controls the universe. And I can better rest in His sovereign hand, which permitted my anxiety in the first place, with the knowledge that He can and will use my trials to conform me into Christ's image.

14. A paraphrase of Jeremiah Burroughs, *The Rare Jewel of Christian Contentment* (Edinburgh: Banner of Truth Trust, 1964), 63.
15. Burroughs, 63.

What an amazing opportunity we have to draw near to God and encounter His peace as we pray!

PRAYER

Dear heavenly Father, my heart grows anxious easily. And I make my anxiety worse by trying to control my life instead of living for You and Your kingdom. If You knew my problems and didn't care, You would be cold and unloving. If You cared but didn't have the power to work in me, You would be unhelpful. Thank You for being almighty God as well as my loving heavenly Father who knows me, cares for me, and works in me. Help me to trust in You more, grow in humility, and abound in thanksgiving. In Jesus's name, amen.

QUESTIONS FOR REFLECTION

1. When has anxiety impeded your prayer life? What did it look like? How did you overcome these challenges?
2. What are some wrong views we may have about God that may increase our anxiety? How might remembering that God is our heavenly Father help us to fight anxiety?
3. Which of the six mind-shifts do you need to incorporate into your life the most? Why?
4. Christ is the ultimate example we can look to of someone who honored God in his life—and his prayer—even during challenging situations. (See Matt. 26:36–46.) Who else can you look to for a reminder of God's faithfulness?

9

i'm too busy

"Learning to pray doesn't offer us a less busy life; it offers us a less busy heart. In the midst of outer busyness we can develop an inner quiet." —Paul E. Miller, A Praying Life

The story of Mary and Martha never seemed fair to me. If you don't remember that story, I'll recap it. In Luke 10:38–42, Jesus visits the home of Mary, Martha, and Lazarus. Mary sits at Jesus's feet, soaking in every word of His teaching, while Martha anxiously runs around serving their guests. Eventually, Martha has had enough. I imagine her stomping her feet in frustration and clenching her fists at her sides as she approaches Jesus to tattle: "Lord, do you not care that my sister has left me to serve alone? Tell her then to help me" (v. 40).

Busy people like me often identify with Martha. She is focusing on action and productivity—that's good, isn't it? She's serving others (as Scripture commands us to do, let me remind you), and her sister isn't helping. A classic case of sibling rivalry. Doesn't Martha have a point?

And yet Jesus's response to her is shocking: "Martha, Martha, you are anxious and troubled about many things, but one thing is necessary. Mary has chosen the good portion, which will not be taken away from her" (vv. 41–42).

How does Jesus conclude this? First, we need to note that He doesn't label Martha's busyness as being bad; what He says is that her being "anxious and troubled about many things" is bad—especially in comparison with what is essential: spending time in His presence. Martha was caring more about the work to be done than about enjoying her guest—who just happened to be the long-awaited Messiah and God in the flesh. Nagging her sister for choosing time with Jesus instead of setting the table revealed how misaligned her priorities were.

And yet . . . someone still needed to serve the guests! We can't sit around all day at Jesus's feet . . . or can we? How can we apply the principle of this passage—that our greatest priority is always spending time with Jesus—when our lives are incredibly hectic? That's the question I will answer in this chapter.

I will offer no one-size-fits-all solutions for conquering busyness. My simple hope is that you will desire to connect with God more fully through prayer and will finish the chapter with a better idea of how you can invite Him into the busyness and everydayness of your life. And don't worry—I'll keep this chapter to the point. I know you're busy.

Let's look first at the reasons (and potential idols) that lie behind our busyness.

WHY ARE WE SO BUSY?

We are busy because . . .

. . . We Want Our Lives to Count

Most Christians realize that couch potatoes rarely accomplish much for the kingdom. After all, Jesus taught that "whoever loses

his life for my sake and the gospel's will save it" (Mark 8:35)—
and so pouring out our lives for the gospel's sake is the best way
for us to live.

. . . Busyness Is Necessary

Parents of young children know what I'm talking about. So
do people who work in a demanding profession or hold multiple
jobs. Students know the challenge of busyness as well—balancing
a full load in school with an internship, church participation, and
a social life is tough. Sometimes you don't choose the busy life;
it chooses you.

. . . We Are Proud

Many people answer the question "How are you?" with
"Busy"—something that they wear as a status symbol. We want
people to like us, to think that we're important and worth the air
we breathe, and so we post about our busyness on social media.[1]
We think that the world will fall apart if we can't attend to our
urgent tasks and do it on our timetable—not realizing that thinking this way makes us lose sight of the One who holds the world
together (see Col. 1:17).

. . . We Fear Missing Out

We looked at the FOMO phenomenon in chapter 6. Our fear
of missing out not only robs our focus but also robs our time.
We covet the vacations, social media feeds, and possessions of
others, causing us to spend countless hours scheming about how
to get what we want. People of other generations simply called

---

1. One experiment found that people who post often on social media about being
busy are considered by those in the United States to be of a higher status. See Joe Pin-
sker, "'Ugh, I'm So Busy': A Status Symbol for Our Time," *The Atlantic*, March 1, 2017,
https://www.theatlantic.com/business/archive/2017/03/busyness-status-symbol
/518178/.

FOMO "discontent"—and this discontent sneakily robs our mental energy from the more important, more renewing activities of life such as prayer.

... We Don't Establish Boundaries for Our Technology

Modern technology seeks to intrude into every nook and cranny of our schedules (as we saw in chapter 6 as well). A lack of discipline regarding our devices means that more of our time is wasted and often makes us think we have less time for seeking God than we actually do.

... We Are Avoiding Deeper Issues

Instead of dealing with major issues in our lives, such as a besetting sin, deep emotional pain, or feelings of rejection, we fill our schedules to the brim with activities—more work, more leisure, more trips to the gym, or more staring at a screen.[2] Pastor Kevin DeYoung warns that "the greatest danger with busyness is that there may be greater dangers you never have time to consider."[3] No one will be able to say, "I was too busy to pray" while they are standing before the judgment seat of God.[4]

And this list is just the beginning of the conversation.

Note that even the good reasons for being busy (such as wanting your life to count) can still bring negative consequences if they make you *too* busy.

Perhaps you know the consequences of being too busy: Your brain is always moving at a million miles an hour from trying to

2. If you are running away from deep issues like this, run to Jesus instead with your deepest pains and insecurities. He knows your pains, struggles, and burdens and will help you and heal you if you give Him the chance.

3. Kevin DeYoung, *Crazy Busy: A (Mercifully) Short Book about a (Really) Big Problem* (Wheaton, IL: Crossway, 2013), 31–32.

4. See Thomas Brooks, *Private Prayer: The Key to Open the Heaven*, ed. Vasile Lazar (1665; repr., Dascălu-Ilfov, Romania: Magna Gratia Ministries, 2017), 91.

juggle a to-do list that is too long, too urgent, and around here somewhere.... Your activities sometimes lack joy—but never stress. You're tired, and your busyness is even affecting your health and the lives of those around you.[5] If this is you, then you're a Martha.

"It's hard to love when you're in a hurry," a busy believer confessed to me. And since we are called to love God and others, our busyness could pose major problems for us and for others. Wisdom will help us to prioritize what is essential and what is too much—since there are always more activities for us to commit to than activities that we can fulfill. Humility will help us to recognize when an idol is lurking behind our busyness and will also help us to repent and to rest on God's grace.

Now that we've examined why our lives are so busy and how this can affect us, we're ready to learn ways that we can prioritize prayer when our schedules are full.

ESSENTIAL TACTICS FOR LEADING A BUSY-BUT-PRAYING LIFE

As you walk through the six tactics I share below, you'll notice how ordinary and obvious they seem. They seem that way because they are that way. Growing in prayer isn't about secret formulas or rocket science; it's about being intentional to seek God because you want to know Him and please Him more. May these tactics deepen your desire for God and equip you for seeking Him.

Tactic 1: Plan Time for Both Daily Prayer and Extended Prayer Sessions

One woman I surveyed shared this insight: "It just struck me that I make a daily date with my employer to get paid, with my

---

5. One study says that kids with parents who "work odd or long hours are more likely to evince behavioral or cognitive problems, or be obese." Judith Shulevitz, "Why You Never See Your Friends Anymore," *The Atlantic*, November 2019, https://www

coffee pot to get caffeine and comfort, and even with Facebook to virtually connect with people (on a superficial level at best)—but I don't do the same for my Father who loves me. . . . Things that make you go 'hmmmm.'"

Hmmmm indeed! And yet I can relate. I bet you can, too. That's why we need to plan.

Building prayer into your daily schedule will make it more natural and automatic. Daily prayer and Bible reading lay the foundation of our relationship with God and keep us abiding in Him instead of running on spiritual fumes. If you've reached this point in the book, you already know about my own personal practices in this area; so I'll share two recommendations from other people that I've found helpful—one from a sixteenth-century Reformer and another from a modern-day business lawyer. Both people found ways to incorporate prayer into their busy lives.

John Calvin recommended praying at special times throughout the day, during which "all the devotion of the heart should be completely engaged"—specifically "when we arise in the morning, before we begin daily work, when we sit down to a meal, when by God's blessing we have eaten, when we are getting ready to retire."[6] He warned, though, against implementing this routine in a superstitious or legalistic way; it should be done as a discipline in order to strengthen us through exercise and repetition.[7]

Justin Whitmel Earley is a lawyer in Richmond, Virginia, who recommends kneeling to pray at morning, midday, and bedtime.[8] He suggests taking a kneeling posture because it serves as a physical reminder of our humility before God and because "I need

.theatlantic.com/magazine/archive/2019/11/why-dont-i-see-you-anymore/598336/.

6. See *Calvin: Institutes of the Christian Religion*, vol. 2, *Books III.XX to IV.XX*, ed. John T. McNeill, trans. Ford Lewis Battles (Philadelphia: The Westminster Press, 1960), 3.20.50.

7. Calvin, 3.20.50.

8. See Justin Whitmel Earley, *The Common Rule: Habits of Purpose for an Age of Distraction* (Downers Grove, IL: IVP Books, 2019), 41.

something physical to mark the moment for my slippery mind."[9] When in his office, he will shut his door at midday and kneel to reframe his day, by focusing on his purpose of loving God and loving others through his work. "The habit always interrupts things in the best of ways. By introducing a new habit, there's a hook in each day, a place where the focus on self is snagged and disrupted. And I'm reminded that work is not for me but for someone else, so I can turn the rest of my workday toward that someone, whether a client, customer, employee, or stranger."[10]

We should also seek to spend *extended times* in prayer when possible. An extended time might be as long as a weeklong retreat or as short as a half hour. One of my seminary professors gave the students in our class a choice between writing a final paper or spending eight straight hours in prayer. I chose prayer, and it was a great decision—and not just because I was burned out by papers! My prayer time refreshed me. I went beyond all my normal, daily prayer requests and prayed with an open Bible, responded to the Word, and pondered God's love. I reflected on the grace He has shown in my life and the people He's had me cross paths with. And I prayed for them. I prayed for my sanctification. I walked my neighborhood and continued my conversation with God. The eight hours passed quickly, and I could have kept going! God had renewed my spirits after a draining semester.

Pull out a calendar and see when and how you can build in pockets of time for communing with God. If your schedule is too jam-packed with commitments, look for ways to build margins into what you're already doing. This might be as simple as scheduling in ten minutes to catch your breath and pray between commitments. Doing so adds a healthy buffer to your constant onslaught of activity and helps your mind to catch up on all that you have done throughout the day and hope to do.

9. Earley, 14.
10. Earley, 41.

Tactic 2: Plan Solitude

Jesus instructed us in Matthew 6:6 to, "when you pray, go into your room and shut the door and pray to your Father who is in secret. And your Father who sees in secret will reward you." And He modeled what He taught. He had a demanding ministry that involved people who always wanted a piece of Him, and yet He fought to spend time alone with the Father. After feeding the five thousand in Mark 6:30–44, Jesus "immediately . . . made his disciples get into the boat and go before him to the other side, to Bethsaida, while he dismissed the crowd. And after he had taken leave of them, he went up to the mountain to pray" (vv. 45–46).

After having *just* performed the miracle of feeding the five thousand, Jesus now did the equivalent of when a youth pastor flickers the lights after youth group to tell kids it's time to go home. Why? Because even though He was fully God and fully human, He needed time to commune with His Father. *Alone.*

You may not have a mountain to run off to for solitude and prayer, but you can incorporate solitude into your life in other ways. I spent every spring break during college in Daytona Beach, Florida, with a group from my school seeking to evangelize spring breakers. It turns out that handing out free cheeseburgers can open the door to many great gospel conversations! And yet finding time for the Word and prayer was a challenge for me on these trips, with its early mornings, late nights, and lack of privacy in a room that I shared with four other college guys. So, during the day when I needed spiritual strength, I'd escape to a one-person public bathroom nearby, lock the door, and pray.

Susanna Wesley, mother of the evangelist John Wesley and the hymn writer Charles Wesley, had an incredibly busy life running the Wesley household, which included ten children. Desperate to seek solitude with the Lord, she would sit in a favorite chair with her Bible and pull her apron over her face. This symbolically cut her off from her children and the world, thereby giving her privacy to commune with her Lord. Her kids quickly learned to not bother Mom when her apron was covering her face![11]

Tactic 3: When Possible, Plan the Place

While true worshippers can pray anywhere in spirit and in truth (see John 4:21–24), some settings are more conducive to prayer than others. That's why Jesus advised going into your room and shutting the door when you pray (see Matt. 6:6).

"I have some of the best and most joyful prayer in my car in the morning on my forty-five-minute commute to work," my sister Kelly told me. "There is something about being in a silent car, with all other distractions removed, that makes the prayers just flow. I feel joy during these prayer times being still before God, talking to Him, and listening to His voice." I find that praying during my own commute can be hit or miss. It usually helps if I warm up my heart with the Word and prayer before I begin the commute, or else I struggle to focus.

No matter whether it's a car, a mountain, a bathroom, a private office, an apron, or a special devotions chair (as we saw in chapter 6), the right place can lead to great prayer. Find your place (or places), and pray away!

Tactic 4: Discover the Power of Short, Faith-Filled Prayers

Remember that God does not hear your prayers because of their length or your eloquent words; He hears them because you're His blood-bought child and He's your gracious Father. That means that God hears your prayers if they're ten thousand words long or if they're only one. "True prayer is measured by weight, and not by length," wrote Charles Spurgeon. "A single

11. See Jackie Green and Lauren Green-McAfee, "The Praying Example of Susanna Wesley," FaithGateway, HarperCollins Christian Publishing, June 5, 2018, https://www.faithgateway.com/praying-example-susanna-wesley/#.YK5ao5NKiCc.

groan before God may have more fulness of prayer in it than a fine oration of great length."[12]

It may surprise you how short many of the Bible's prayers are. The Lord's Prayer takes about twenty seconds to pray. Paul's prayers range from taking about two seconds to pray to taking about seventy-five seconds.[13] You can pray the prayer of Jabez (see 1 Chron. 4:10) and the shortest of the psalms (Ps. 117) in about ten seconds or less.[14] There are many times that we don't have a chance for longer prayers. And that's fine. Your heavenly Father welcomes any. Nehemiah "prayed to the God of heaven" (Neh. 2:4) in the middle of an important conversation,[15] and while we don't know the content of his short prayer, we do know that God answered it.

I've found that there is benefit in pausing throughout the day to offer up to God a short, heartfelt prayer and to trust that He hears me. This adds a richness to my walk with God, the way a simple text from my wife that says "love you" reminds me of our special relationship.

While you are enjoying a beautiful sunset, a pleasant breeze, or another part of God's creation, draw your heart to God's by saying "Thanks!" or "Wow! That's amazing." When you are discouraged, pray "I need You to strengthen me"—or simply cry "Father!" or "Help!" We build relationships every day through short conversations that we have by text message and social media. Why would our heavenly Father reject any short prayer from a child whom He loves so dearly?[16]

---

12. Charles Haddon Spurgeon, *Encouraged to Pray: Classic Sermons on Prayer* (n.p.: Cross-Points, 2017), 31.

13. The shortest of his prayers is at the end of Titus 3:15, and the longest covers Colossians 1:3–14.

14. The prayer of Jabez sometimes gets a bad rap because some people abuse it to try to achieve worldly blessing. But I believe it can be prayed in line with the rest of scriptural truth—and for great benefit. It is inspired Scripture, after all!

15. Notice also his longer prayer in Nehemiah 1:5–11.

16. We do have to make a necessary caveat about short prayers: they don't take the place of longer and deeper times of prayer—just as I don't only communicate with my

As we pepper our busy lives with short, faith-filled prayers, we grow in God's will and learn to "pray without ceasing" (1 Thess. 5:17; see also v. 18).

Tactic 5: Habit Stack Your Prayers

"Habit stacking" is a term coined by James Clear to describe a simple idea: that the easiest way to start a new habit is to tack it on to an existing habit that you already have. That way, the new habit can start with the momentum in place from an older one that's already automatic. The ridiculously simple formula for habit stacking is "After [CURRENT HABIT], I will [NEW HABIT]."[17] That's it. You probably already do this—even relating to prayer. If you pause to thank God for your food after sitting down to eat, you habit stack. The same is true if you pray for your kids after tucking them into bed or pray for safety after loading up your car for a road trip.

I've intentionally sought ways to invite God into my normal activities through habit stacking. When I open a bill, I thank God for providing the service that I'm paying for and for the funds to pay it. When a friend asks me for prayer, I pray then and there. When I see a police cruiser drive by with its siren on, I pray for peace, justice, and safety to prevail for all who are involved in the emergency. Before I start a meeting, I pray as well.

How can you tie prayer to an existing habit? Perhaps when you begin your work, you can pray for the Lord to help you work for His glory and to bless the work of your hands. Perhaps when you shower, you can bring a Ziploc bag with you containing a notecard with a Scripture verse to meditate on and a few requests to pray over. Perhaps before you turn on the TV with your family, you can first spend five minutes in prayer together.

wife via text. We need time for deeper conversations as well.

17. James Clear, *Atomic Habits: An Easy & Proven Way to Build Good Habits & Break Bad Ones* (New York: Avery, 2018), 74. The apostle Paul practiced this, as well, with this formula: After [I think of the Philippians], I will [thank God for them] (Phil. 1:3).

The opportunities for injecting your life with joy by focusing on God through prayer are literally endless. You may even find—as I routinely do—that habit-stacked small prayers lead to deeper and longer times in prayer.

Tactic 6: Rest

The best way to grow in prayer may not be planning prayer but planning rest. Building rest into our schedules often results in inner peace and restored mental energy—much as rebooting a computer helps it to run more smoothly by cleaning out the digital cobwebs. Tim Keller writes, "To rest is actually a way to enjoy and honor the goodness of God's creation and our own. To violate the rhythm of work and rest (in either direction) leads to chaos in our life and in the world around us. Sabbath is therefore a celebration of our design."[18]

Theologian John Stott learned early in his ministry to schedule one day a month to be a "quiet day" that allowed him space for prayer, reading, and long-term planning. He recorded that these relaxed and restful days "brought immense blessing to [his] life and ministry" and lifted off him an "intolerable burden" of activity.[19]

How can you use rest to recharge your spiritual batteries?

DID MARTHA LEARN HER LESSON?

We know little about Martha's life after the incident that opened this chapter—including whether she learned her lesson. I think

18. Tim Keller, "The Power of Deep Rest," The Gospel Coalition, November 25, 2012, https://www.thegospelcoalition.org/article/the-power-of-deep-rest/.

19. John Stott, *The Challenge of Preaching*, abridged and updated by Greg Scharf (2013; repr., Grand Rapids: William B. Eerdmans, 2015), 48. See also Kevin Halloran, "John Stott's Simple Secret for Spiritual Productivity," *Anchored in Christ* (blog), August 1, 2016, https://www.kevinhalloran.net/john-stotts-simple-yet-surprising-spiritual-productivity-secret/.

that she did. If she loved Jesus, then she loved truth—even truth that comes in the form of a rebuke.

Let's imagine ten years have passed since Jesus rebuked her. Jesus has since died and risen from the dead. (And so has her brother Lazarus.) Jesus has also ascended into heaven. (Lazarus hasn't.) Martha, Mary, and Lazarus worship the risen Messiah together as part of the same church: First Church of the Resurrection in Bethany.

Martha has agreed to have her growing church over for worship and a meal on the Lord's day, and she begins to stress. There's just so much to do—and this time it really is up to her. As she looks ahead to a couple of busy days of preparation, she strategizes how she can commune with the Lord and not run herself ragged. "Lord, help me to be wise!" she prays. Martha knows that she will have to postpone or cancel a couple of commitments, and so she does. She also plans a relaxed morning for the following week, when she can sleep in and spend extra time seeking God. As she thinks about the days ahead, she commits to praying each time stress creeps up on her. She even chooses Psalm 23 to be her theme passage that she will meditate on during her chores, and so far it has brought her much joy in her Savior.

"Father, thank you for sending Jesus," she prays. "Instead of letting my to-do list overwhelm me, I'm going to give each step of the preparations to you and thank You for your physical and spiritual provision and for giving me the energy to serve. Please help me to worship You as I prepare for this gathering, and keep me from feeling overwhelmed. This time I will choose the good portion."

PRAYER

Father, You of all people know my busy schedule and busy heart. I pray that You would increase my desire to commune with You throughout the day. I need Your help with growing in faith, discipline, and intentionality in my walk with You. And, Father, I thank You for Your abundant grace and listening ear and that the efficacy of my prayers is based not on their length or eloquence but on the fact that I'm Your child because of the finished work of Jesus. Please help me to live more and more in awe of Your extravagant grace. In Jesus's name, amen.

QUESTIONS FOR REFLECTION

1. Do you consider yourself to be too busy? If so, which of the reasons in this chapter for why we're busy most apply to you?
2. How might you intentionally plan for prayer (in terms of time, solitude, or a location) as you move forward?
3. What are some ways you can habit stack prayer?
4. How well do you rest from your busy life? In what way might resting more intentionally help you to pray?

conclusion:
the struggle is worth it

Several years have passed since I began examining why I struggled to pray. To say that doing so has been an illuminating and rewarding journey would be an understatement. I'm still not the world's best pray-er, and I still struggle at times with forgetfulness or focus or the other issues we have explored in this book—but my journey has equipped me to push through such struggles and to pray on, with my eyes on our gracious God.

Hopefully, as you've read *When Prayer Is a Struggle*, God has helped you to see the point of the book: that every Christian can experience more joyful and effective prayer by facing their struggles with prayer head-on. The goal of doing so isn't perfection (because we'll never reach it!); it's faithfulness and progress. And, by God's grace and with the help of His church, we can pray more faithfully, bear fruit through our prayers, and—most importantly—grow in our knowledge of God Himself.

We've worked through the nine common prayer struggles:

- Chapter 1 looked at a foundational struggle: that we forget why prayer matters. It reminded us that we pray because we want God's name to be glorified, His kingdom to be expanded, His will to be realized, His provision to be experienced, His forgiveness to be treasured, and His protection to be granted.

- Chapter 2 showed us that when we do not know what to say while praying, there are many paths we can take to pursue fruitful and focused prayer—chief among which are praying based on, or responding to, God's Word.
- Chapter 3 applied the gospel to guilty hearts and helped us to see guilt as a motivator—not a detriment—to prayer.
- Chapter 4 explored why God may seem silent when we pray and encouraged us to confide in Him and His eternal purposes.
- Chapter 5 diagnosed our wrong motives for praying and encouraged us to pray on, even when we are unsure of our motives.
- Chapter 6 tackled our lack of focus in prayer and suggested many practical ways we can fight distraction.
- Chapter 7 taught that we should take all of God's commands regarding prayer seriously and also shared several methods for organizing our prayers and intercessions to make them more intentional and well-rounded.
- Chapter 8 helped us to see how (and how not) to battle anxiety through prayer and how to enjoy the peace that God grants His children.
- Chapter 9 shared ways that we can pursue lives of prayer when our schedules are crazy.

Now we come to perhaps the most important six words of this book:

What will you do about it?

I mean this question not in a beating-you-over-the-head, legalistic way, but as a realistic warning. Reading a book like this without attempting to put it into practice not only is a waste of time but also reveals a heart that is cold toward God.

I don't expect you to remember and practice all I have covered or suggested in this book, and God doesn't either. My recommendation is that you think of the top two or three prayer-related struggles that you face and then focus on growing in those areas. Then, when you face one of the other nine struggles in the future, pull this book off your shelf and refresh your memory regarding how to move forward.

A key goal I have for my own prayer is simply to have a never-give-up attitude. This attitude comes from a parable that Jesus told in Luke 18. Luke was kind enough to introduce this parable by sharing the purpose for it: "And he told them a parable to the effect that they *ought always to pray and not lose heart*" (v. 1).

> In a certain city there was a judge who neither feared God nor respected man. And there was a widow in that city who kept coming to him and saying, "Give me justice against my adversary." For a while he refused, but afterward he said to himself, "Though I neither fear God nor respect man, yet because this widow keeps bothering me, I will give her justice, so that she will not beat me down by her continual coming." . . . Hear what the unrighteous judge says. And will not God give justice to his elect, who cry to him day and night? Will he delay long over them? I tell you, he will give justice to them speedily. Nevertheless, when the Son of Man comes, will he find faith on earth? (vv. 2–8)

The point of the parable lies in the contrast it sets up. The unjust judge eventually responded to the widow's persistent pleading because he was annoyed. But God the Father doesn't get annoyed by His beloved children, and so we can trust that He will not delay in responding to us. He will answer.

The way Jesus closes the parable in verse 8 might seem random: "When the Son of Man comes, will he find faith on earth?"

But as we saw in this book's introduction, faith is a necessary part of true, God-pleasing prayer. Faith prays and doesn't give up.

So don't give up seeking God through prayer, brother or sister in Christ. Life is short. Yours will go by in the blink of an eye. God is worth pursuing with all that you have, and His gospel is worth giving your life for.

Will you lose heart, or will you pray?

acknowledgments

I've always heard how creating a book is a team effort, and now I know it from experience.

First, praise and worship are due to the God and Father of our Lord Jesus Christ. He graciously saved me from my sin, made me His son, and invites me to pray. He also planted the seed for *When Prayer Is a Struggle* in my heart years ago, answered dozens (if not hundreds or even thousands) of my prayers throughout the process of creating this book, and provided the rest of the wonderful people who helped to make this book possible.

Next up in order of importance is my beautiful and loving wife, Jazlynn. Thank you for your love, faith, patience, encouragement, wisdom, and friendship that have been a rock to me. I look forward to continuing to deepen our love and gospel partnership in all areas of life. And while little Sadie doesn't yet understand her contribution to this book, I thank her for patience in letting Dada write the many times when playing or cuddling seemed more expedient. Sadie, you bring so much joy to my life. My deepest desire for you is that you will know and love Jesus, too.

I owe thanks to my parents for their examples as faithful prayer warriors as well as to other family members, friends, and colleagues for their encouragement and the helpful comments and critiques they contributed to initial drafts of this book. Your words are more gracious than I deserved, and they made this book much stronger.

Thank you to the staff at WordPartners. You encouraged me in this work and continue to deepen my love for God and His Word through the biblical vision you have for ministry, humility, God-centeredness, and love for one another. It was a tremendous privilege to serve God and His kingdom alongside you.

Thank you to The Orchard Evangelical Free Church, for your commitment to praying, singing, and preaching God's Word, and to Pastor Colin Smith, whose theological fingerprints are all over this book—and my life. I'd also like to thank the Unlocking the Bible team, for their continual encouragement, and all who took the informal surveys on my blog, *Anchored in Christ* (www.kevin-halloran.net), which helped to shape this book.

And lastly, a big thanks to Dave Almack and the whole crew at P&R Publishing for your encouragement, hard work, and belief in this idea.

But truly God has listened;
he has attended to the voice of my prayer. (Ps. 66:19)

Kevin Halloran
Soli Deo Gloria

appendix: select prayers from scripture

One of the best ways to pray is with an open Bible. This appendix shares a few helpful starting points for praying Scripture.

SELECT PSALMS BY TOPIC OR SITUATION

Psalms for Anxiety, Fear, and Depression
23, 27, 34, 42, 43, 46, 55, 56, 61, 62, 91

Psalms of Comfort
16, 23, 116, 119

Psalms of Confession and Repentance
32, 38, 51

Psalms for Deliverance and Protection
5, 6, 7, 31, 34, 35, 40, 41, 55, 59, 60, 91, 116, 121, 140, 142

Psalms of Faith and Trust
31, 62, 118, 125, 130, 143

Psalms for General Praise and Worship
29, 93, 95, 96, 100, 103, 107, 111, 115, 117, 135, 136, 139, 145, 150

Psalms on God's Word
1, 19, 119

Psalms for Guidance
23, 25, 86, 143

Psalms of Lament
5, 12, 13, 22, 31, 42, 51, 74, 80, 88

Psalms Praising God for Creation
8, 19, 33, 104, 148

Psalms for Strength
28, 46, 63, 73, 89, 105, 118

Psalms of Thanksgiving
9, 28, 30, 69, 92, 95, 100, 105, 107, 118, 136, 138, 147

Psalms for When the Wicked Prosper
2, 10, 37, 49, 73

SELECT PRAYERS FROM THE APOSTLE PAUL BY THEME

We can use the following prayers from the apostle Paul to shape and stir prayers of our own.

Knowing and Praising God
Ephesians 1:15–23
Ephesians 3:14–21
Colossians 1:3–14
1 Timothy 1:17

Spiritual Growth
Romans 15:5–6
Romans 15:13
1 Corinthians 1:4–9
2 Corinthians 1:3–11
2 Corinthians 13:7–9
2 Corinthians 13:14
Philippians 1:3–6
Philippians 1:9–11
Philippians 4:6–7
1 Thessalonians 1:2–3
1 Thessalonians 2:13–16
1 Thessalonians 3:9–13
1 Thessalonians 5:23–24
2 Thessalonians 1:3–4
2 Thessalonians 1:11–12
2 Thessalonians 2:16–17
2 Thessalonians 3:16

Gospel Ministry
Romans 15:30–33
2 Corinthians 2:14–16
2 Corinthians 9:12–15
Ephesians 6:18–20
Colossians 4:2–4
2 Thessalonians 3:1–5
1 Timothy 2:1–6
Philemon 4–7

suggested resources for going deeper in prayer

RECOMMENDED BOOKS ON PRAYER

Boa, Kenneth. *Face to Face*. 2 vols. Grand Rapids: Zondervan, 1997. [Boa curates Scriptures for daily prayer and worship.]

Calvin, John. *The Chief Exercise of Faith: John Calvin on Prayer*. Translated by Henry Beveridge. N.p.: Cross-Points, 2018. [A stand-alone volume of the chapter from the *Institutes of the Christian Religion* in which Calvin offers a rich treatment of prayer that is theological, practical, short, and fairly comprehensive. That's why men such as J. I. Packer, R.C. Sproul, and Tim Keller have expressed a deep appreciation for it.]

Carson, D. A. *Praying with Paul: A Call to Spiritual Reformation*. Grand Rapids: Baker Academic, 2015. [A renowned theologian with a pastor's heart masterfully teaches through the prayers of the great apostle. This has my highest recommendation.]

Guthrie, Nancy. *The One Year Praying through the Bible for Your Kids*. Carol Stream, IL: Tyndale Momentum, 2016. [A helpful guide for parents as they pray for their kids.]

Hunter, W. Bingham. *The God Who Hears.* Downers Grove, IL: IVP Books, 1986. [A former seminary professor unpacks, in an accessible, practical, and inspiring way, why God wants us to pray.]

Luther, Martin. *A Simple Way to Pray.* Louisville: Westminster John Knox Press, 2000. Reprint, St. Louis: Concordia Publishing House, 2012. [Luther wrote this short and immensely practical book for his barber, who wanted instruction on how to pray. These thirty pages will do more for your prayer life than most entire books on prayer. Search the internet for free digital versions.]

Miller, Paul E. *A Praying Life: Connecting with God in a Distracting World.* Rev. ed. Colorado Springs: NavPress, 2017. [A modern-day classic that will help you to invite God into the daily grind and difficulties of life. I know of no book that will warm your heart to pray like this one will.]

Patterson, Ben. *God's Prayer Book: The Power and Pleasure of Praying the Psalms.* Carol Stream, IL: SaltRiver, 2008. [Patterson provides rich teaching in this book's introduction and spends the rest of the book unpacking how selected psalms can inspire us to pray. This is my top recommendation for someone who wants a model to follow for praying the Psalms.]

Spurgeon, Charles Haddon. *Encouraged to Pray: Classic Sermons on Prayer.* N.p.: Cross-Points, 2017. [Rich, deep, thoroughly biblical, and pithy. Exactly what you'd expect from the Prince of Preachers.]

Wax, Trevin. *Psalms in 30 Days: A Prayer Guide through the Psalter.* Nashville: Holman Bible Publishers, 2020. [Wax walks through three psalms a day, in a morning, midday, and evening pattern, and shares accompanying prayers from faithful believers. A great resource to provide structure for your praying.]

Westlund, Kathi Lambrides. *Prayer PathWay: Journeying in a Life of Prayer*. Phillipsburg, NJ: P&R Publishing, 2016. [Westlund offers practical guidance on praying Scripture as well as space for journaling.]

Whitney, Donald S. *Praying the Bible*. Wheaton, IL: Crossway, 2015. [This short book by Whitney explores a simple and powerful method for using Scripture to guide your prayers.]

———. *Spiritual Disciplines for the Christian Life*. Rev. and updated ed. Colorado Springs: NavPress, 2014. [This book provides a deep and inspirational look at the what, why, and how of pursuing God through prayer and other spiritual disciplines.]

SUGGESTED RESOURCES ON SPECIALTY TOPICS

DeYoung, Kevin. *Crazy Busy: A (Mercifully) Short Book about a (Really) Big Problem*. Wheaton, IL: Crossway, 2013. [DeYoung diagnoses our busyness and engages our hearts with Scripture in witty fashion.]

Hansen, Collin, and John Woodbridge. *A God-Sized Vision: Revival Stories That Stretch and Stir*. Grand Rapids: Zondervan, 2010. [Hansen, a journalist, and Woodbridge, a professor of church history (as well as my own former professor), document seven historical revivals that took place across four continents. Read this book to expand your vision of how God has used prayer to work on a grand scale.]

Mandryk, Jason. *Operation World: The Definitive Prayer Guide to Every Nation*. 7th ed. Reprint, Downers Grove, IL: IVP Books, 2010. [This thousand-page reference will teach you how to pray specific prayers for each nation in the world. There is an abridged version called *Pray for the World* that came out in 2015.]

Piper, John. *A Hunger for God: Desiring God through Fasting and Prayer*. Reprint, Wheaton, IL: Crossway, 2013. [The best book on fasting I know. Get the PDF for free at http://www.desiringGod.org/books/a-hunger-for-god.]

Reinke, Tony. *12 Ways Your Phone Is Changing You*. Wheaton, IL: Crossway, 2017. [If you're always on your phone and social media, this book will challenge you and help you to think about technology from a biblical perspective.]

Tautges, Paul. *Anxiety: Knowing God's Peace*. 31-Day Devotionals for Life. Phillipsburg, NJ: P&R Publishing, 2019. [Tautges guides readers to fight anxiety using scriptural truth.]

RECOMMENDED BOOKS OF PRAYERS

Bennett, Arthur, ed. *The Valley of Vision: A Collection of Puritan Prayers and Devotions*. Edinburgh: Banner of Truth Trust, 1975. [This much-beloved classic allows readers to pray rich, gospel-centered prayers along with saints of old, such as John Bunyan, Thomas Watson, Charles Spurgeon, Isaac Watts, and others.]

Duguid, Barbara R., and Wayne Duguid Houk. *Prone to Wander: Prayers of Confession and Celebration*. Edited by Iain M. Duguid. Phillipsburg, NJ: P&R Publishing, 2014. [Inspired by *The Valley of Vision*, this book offers prayers of confession that celebrate the gospel.]

Henry, Matthew. *A Method for Prayer: Freedom in the Face of God*. Edited and revised by J. Ligon Duncan III. Fearn, UK: Christian Focus Publications, 1994. [Ligon Duncan updated the language of this classic to make it more accessible to modern readers. Each page is packed with prayers that will move your heart. It is so rich that I have a hard time reading more than one page at a time!]

Smith, Scotty. *Everyday Prayers: 365 Days to a Gospel-Centered Faith.* Grand Rapids: Baker Books, 2011. [Pray biblical and honest prayers along with Pastor Scotty Smith in this volume that shares prayers that were originally posted on Smith's blog, which has been described as "a tutorial for gospel praying."]

Also well worth consulting is the *Book of Common Prayer*, which has been a staple for generations of Anglicans as well as other believers. This resource leads readers through prayers and portions of Scripture for many occasions.

Kevin P. Halloran (MDiv, Trinity Evangelical Divinity School) serves with Unlocking the Bible—a ministry dedicated to proclaiming Christ through media, mobilizing believers for evangelism, and equipping leaders for the church. Kevin lives near Chicago, Illinois, with his wife and daughter. Visit www.kevinhalloran.net to read his writing and connect with him on social media.

Did you find this book helpful?
Consider leaving a review online.
The author appreciates your feedback!

Or write to P&R at editorial@prpbooks.com
with your comments. We'd love to hear from you.

other prayer resources from p&r publishing

Across this four-volume series, beautiful poetic prayers by author Kathleen Nielson address the spiritual well-being, physical needs, and character growth of a child from infancy to adulthood. Designed for parents, each book has thirty-one prayers, brief reflections, and Scripture selections for meditation.

ALSO IN THE SERIES

Prayers of a Parent for Teens
Prayers of a Parent for Young Adults
Prayers of a Parent for Adult Children

other prayer resources from p&r publishing

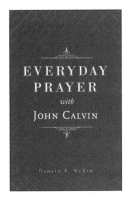
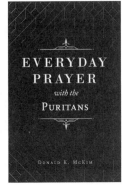
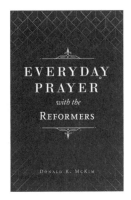

THREE TREASURES OF CLASSIC WISDOM ON PRAYER

The wisdom of John Calvin, the Puritans, and the Reformers shines forth in their teaching on prayer. Drawing from their writings, Donald McKim provides brief, meditative readings with insights to nourish our prayer lives today.

"[Donald McKim] offer[s] us not only well-earned wisdom and sensible encouragement on prayer but also gentle questions to make sure we are making connections ourselves. His goal is not merely to teach us more about prayer but to help us actually to pray! McKim does not overwhelm but offers just enough to point us in the right direction and get us started. I hope it encourages you as it did me." —**Kelly M. Kapic**

other prayer resources from p&r publishing

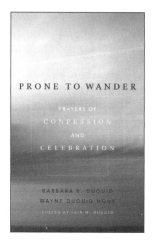 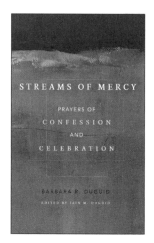

Inspired by the Puritan classic *The Valley of Vision*, the prayers in these two volumes are ideal for use in church services or personal devotions. They open with a scriptural call of confession, confess specific sins, thank the Father for Jesus' perfect life and death in our place, ask for the help of the Spirit in pursuing holiness, and close with an assurance of pardon.

"[*Prone to Wander*] covers the whole of the Christian life. I love its overall aims and method." —**Leland Ryken**

"[In *Streams of Mercy*] we learn how to pray God's Word back to him . . . and celebrate his grace in so many areas of our lives. I recommend strongly." —**John Frame**